# Eternal Feminines

*Mason Welch Gross Lecture Series*

# Eternal Feminines

THREE THEOLOGICAL

ALLEGORIES IN DANTE'S *PARADISO*

## Jaroslav Pelikan

*Rutgers University Press*

NEW BRUNSWICK AND LONDON

Library of Congress Cataloging-in-Publication Data

Pelikan, Jaroslav Jan, 1923–
Eternal feminines : three theological allegories in Dante's
Paradiso / Jaroslav Pelikan.
p.   cm. — (Mason Welch Gross lectures for 1989)
Includes bibliographical references.
ISBN 0-8135-1602-1 (cloth)   ISBN 0-8135-1603-X (pbk.)
1. Dante Alighieri, 1265–1321. Paradiso.   2. Portinari, Beatrice,
1266–1290, in fiction, drama, poetry, etc.   3. Mary, Blessed Virgin,
Saint, in literature.   4. Catholic Church in literature.
5. Christian art and symbolism in literature.   I. Title.
II. Series: Mason Welch Gross lectureship series.
PQ4452.P45   1990
851'.1—dc20                                          90-8261
                                                          CIP

British Cataloging in Publication information available

TO ANGELO BARTLETT GIAMATTI—
MY FAVORITE *DANTISTA*,
AND NOW IMPRESARIO OF THE
*ANGELICI LUDI*
(*PAR*.XXVIII.126)

# Contents

# Preface

UNLIKE many scholars who have written about Dante, I did not begin reading the *Divine Comedy* at an early age. Of George Santayana's "three philosophical poets," it was not Dante (much less Lucretius) on whom I grew up, but Goethe, as the title of this book also reveals. Therefore my first substantial introduction to Dante studies did not come until the lectures of Professor Giuseppe Antonio Borgese during my days as a graduate student at the University of Chicago in the 1940s. (It was also Professor Borgese who introduced me, but in person, to Thomas Mann, who was his father-in-law.) Although from then on I continued to read Dante and about Dante, my next strong stimulus for scholarly attention to him came from a close study of Etienne Gilson's *Dante the Philosopher*, which had appeared in French as *Dante et la philosophie* in 1939 and came out in English ten years later, and which I then had the privilege of discussing with Professor Gilson in person on several occasions. During my early years on the Yale faculty, John Freccero enlightened me on many questions of Dante interpretation, particularly on the complexity of Dante's relation to Augustine.

Most of all, however, I am indebted for my appreciation of the *Divine Comedy* to the *Dantista* in whose memory this book is dedicated, my friend and Yale colleague Angelo Bartlett Giamatti, the late commissioner of baseball. In the academic year 1979/80, when he was already president of Yale, we taught a seminar together on Dante and Aquinas, which set me to serious investigation of Dante's theology; for this, my constant *maestro*, as A. Bartlett Giamatti also used to call him, was Professor Thomas G. Bergin. In the academic year 1985/86 I returned to the topic, joining this time with my colleague Professor Paolo Valesio, of the Department of Italian at Yale, for a series of public lectures on the *Paradiso* under the auspices of the William Clyde DeVane Professorship. And the gracious invitation of Rutgers University to deliver the Mason Welch Gross Lectures in the autumn of 1989 has made it possible for me, after these many years of research, to put my studies of Dante into publishable form in this slender volume. To the original three Mason Welch Gross Lectures, which as Chapters 3–5 are the core of the book, I have added the Kathryn Fraser Mackay Lecture at Saint Lawrence University for 1989, adapted for use here as Chapter 2, and a lecture at the Library of Congress symposium "Knowledge and Power" in 1988, adapted as Chapter 6. At the suggestion of their various original sponsors, these chapters have been edited in such a way as to retain as much as possible of their flavor as lectures, and I have correspondingly repressed my natural instincts for footnoting. I owe a special word of thanks to all the students and colleagues whose questions, comments, and criticisms have made this a better book, and specifically to Professors Remigio Ugo Pane, Juliana D'Amato, O.P., and Paolo Valesio and to my student William Caferro.

In writing *Bach Among the Theologians* (Philadelphia: Fortress Press, 1986) I was careful to disclaim any expertise in musicology, and in the Andrew W. Mellon Lectures in the Fine Arts which I gave at the National Gallery of Art, now being published under the title *Imago Dei: The Byzantine Apologia for Icons* (Princeton: Princeton University Press, 1990), I have made the same disclaimer concerning art history, about which I know less than I do about music. Similarly, I need to explain here that I am not, and do not pretend to have become, a Dantista—although, as the saying goes, some of my best friends are. But because Dante Alighieri, like Johann Sebastian

Bach after him and the Byzantine defenders of icons before him, was steeped in the vocabulary and the thought world of Christian doctrine, on which I do claim to speak with some scholarly authority, I am presuming here to venture into the minefield of Dante studies as well, with the same combination of temerity and timidity that has marked, or that at any rate should mark (although it has not always done so), the ventures of Dante scholars into the no less hazardous regions of the history of Christian doctrine.

Of the vast literature in the field, including the several series of *Lectura Dantis* and standard works of reference, I have read more than I have used here, and used more than I have cited here. But for their special contributions to my understanding of many specific issues, there are two books in my bibliography to which I want to call attention (as it happens, the first is by a former colleague and the second by a former student): Marianne Shapiro, *Woman, Earthly and Divine, in the "Comedy" of Dante,* and Barbara Newman, *Sister of Wisdom: St. Hildegard's Theology of the Feminine.* Because the translation of Dante by Allen Mandelbaum is in blank verse and because it has achieved such wide distribution, I have as a rule quoted from it (as well as from his edition of the Italian), although the prose of the translations by Charles S. Singleton and by John D. Sinclair is often able to come closer to the specifically theological sense of Dante. There are likewise several English translations of Boethius available: by "I. T." (originally 1609) in the Loeb Classical Library, by W. T. Cooper, and by V. E. Watts. I have consulted all of them and have quoted Cooper or Watts occasionally, and I have also occasionally used a translation of my own. But generally I have followed "I. T."; for, in the words of H. F. Stewart and E. K. Rand, "the rendering is most exact," and the Elizabethan tone of its language often seems to come closest to that of the rather Ciceronian original. For some of the same reasons I have usually quoted from the Authorized Version of the English Bible, although I have repeatedly found it preferable to quote and translate the Vulgate, which was of course Dante's Bible.

After some hesitation I have decided to leave the dedication
of this book as it stood on 1 September 1989, the day of
A. Bartlett Giamatti's sudden death. On 6 September I had the
honor and the grief of being the speaker at his graveside, concluding with this explanation: "Ever since our seminar, I have
been working on Dante as theologian, and my little book on
that subject will come out next year. I planned to give him the
first copy, and therefore had not told him that I was dedicating
it to him, with the words of the *Paradiso* in which Dante describes how the Blessed Virgin Mary smiles at all 'the games of
the *angeli* [and of Angelo]'—including Gene Autry's California
*Angeli* but all the other teams as well. Well, now Angelo is
learning about all the games of all the *angeli* at first hand."

# Abbreviations

| | |
|---|---|
| *Cons.* | Boethius *Consolation of Philosophy* |
| *Conv.* | Dante *Convivio* [*Convito*] |
| *Enc.Dant.* | *Enciclopedia Dantesca* |
| *Ep.* | Dante *Epistolae* |
| *Inf.* | Dante *Inferno* |
| *Mon.* | Dante *De Monarchia* |
| *OED* | *Oxford English Dictionary* |
| *Par.* | Dante *Paradiso* |
| *Purg.* | Dante *Purgatorio* |
| *S.T.* | Thomas Aquinas *Summa Theologica* |
| *V.N.* | Dante *Vita Nuova* |

# Eternal Feminines

# Prologue: *Tre Donne*

THE climax of Dante's *Paradiso*, indeed of the entire *Divine Comedy*, is the Trinitarian vision of uncreated Light in the final canto:

> In the deep and bright
> essence of that exalted Light, three circles
> appeared to me: they had three different colors,
> but all of them were of the same dimension;
> one circle seemed reflected by the second,
> as rainbow is by rainbow, and the third
> seemed fire breathed equally by those two circles.[1]

That vision has been anticipated in an earlier canto:

> That One and Two and Three who ever lives
> and ever reigns in Three and Two and One,
> not circumscribed and circumscribing all,
> was sung three times by each and all those souls
> with such a melody that it would be
> appropriate reward for every merit.[2]

According to Dante, as well as according to the entire orthodox theological tradition of Augustinian Trinitarianism in

---

[1] *Par.* XXXIII.115–120.
[2] *Par.* XIV.28–33.

which he stood, this worship of God as Trinity affirms that
even when there was no mankind, no creation, indeed no angels, God the Holy Trinity, to whom "both *is* and *are*" can be
accurately applied,[3] already knew, within the mysterious and
unsearchable depths of transcendent Being itself, the relation
between I and Thou, upon which, in turn, all subsequent relations between and among creatures were to be founded. The
Trinitarian perspective is already present in even earlier cantos of the *Paradiso*.[4] The most thoroughly orthodox dogmatic
statement of it appears in the paraphrase of the opening words
of the Nicene Creed in Canto XXIV:

> I believe in one God—sole,
> eternal—He who, motionless, moves all
> the heavens with His love and love for Him
> . . . . . . . . . . . . . . . . . . . . . . . . . . .
> And I believe in three Eternal Persons,
> and these I do believe to be one essence
> so single and threefold as to allow
> both *is* and *are*.[5]

In fact, however, Dante's Trinitarianism is all-pervasive not
only in the *Paradiso*, but throughout the *Divine Comedy*.[6] It
expresses itself already near the very beginning of the poem,
in the inscription over the gate of hell in the *Inferno*, with its
confession that the Holy Trinity of "Divine Authority [the Father as the Source of the entire Godhead and as Creator of
heaven and earth], the Highest Wisdom [the Son of God, as the
Eternal Wisdom through whom the earth was created],[7] and

---

[3] *Par*.XXIV.141.

[4] *Par*.XIII.25–27.

[5] *Par*.XXIV.130–147, words that are echoed in John Henry Newman's *The Dream of Gerontius* (which contains other echoes of Dante as well): "Firmly I believe and truly / God is Three, and God is One."

[6] *Enc.Dant*. 5:718–721.

[7] This is one of only five instances in the entire poem where the word *sapienza* appears.

the Primal Love [the Holy Spirit as, according to Augustine's *On the Trinity*, the *amor* that unites the Father and the Son],"[8] was the "High Artificer" who fashioned this "Suffering City."[9] Although they may not all be intended as explicit references to the Divine Trinity, threes abound in Dante's poem: in the three heads of the vision in Canto XXXII of the *Purgatorio*,[10] in the *tre melode* of the angels' perpetual hosanna,[11] in the apostolic flame that whirls three times around Beatrice,[12] in the three apostles Peter, James, and John in Cantos XXIV–XXVI of the *Paradiso* (for whom Dante named his three sons), and even in the very terza rima of its verse.[13] From the Augustinian tradition Dante learned a Trinitarian hermeneutics, which enabled him both to read the Bible in the light of the Trinity and to find *vestigia Trinitatis* within the self and throughout the universe.

Especially interesting are the several instances of *tre donne*, which appear in all three *cantiche* of the poem as well as elsewhere in Dante's works.[14] Already in Canto II of the *Inferno* Virgil, speaking about Mary, Lucy, and Beatrice as the *tre donne benedette*, chides Dante:

> Where are your daring and your openness
> as long as there are three such blessed women
> concerned for you within the court of Heaven?[15]

Again, in his vision of the Earthly Paradise near the conclusion of the *Purgatorio*, Dante the pilgrim beholds another circle and, within it, another group of three ladies, *tre donne in*

---

[8]Augustine *On the Trinity* XV.xvii.27–31.
[9]*Inf.*III.5–6.
[10]*Purg.*XXXII.144.
[11]*Par.*XXVIII.118–119.
[12]*Par.*XXIV.22.
[13]See Freccero 1986, 260–264.
[14]See Pépin 1970, 122–123.
[15]*Inf.*II.123–125; see the comments of Di Scipio 1984, 105–109.

*giro*.[16] From the explanation of these *tre donne* that is given only much later, in Canto XX of the *Paradiso*,[17] it is evident, as the commentators seem unanimous in suggesting, that these three ladies are an allegorical representation of the theological virtues of faith, hope, and charity—all three of these being, in Dante's Italian no less than in the Church's Latin, feminine nouns.[18] Though not always as *tre donne*, and sometimes as *tre croci*,[19] faith, hope, and charity put in an appearance at other junctures of the *Divine Comedy*—sometimes all in the same sentence, as in the formula that Beatrice employs in her recommendation of Dante to Saint Peter: "He loves well and hopes well and has faith."[20] The most prominent such appearance of the standard triad from 1 Corinthians 13:13 comes in the threefold examination of Dante as a degree candidate in the heavenly Academy, with Saint Peter quizzing him on faith, Saint James on hope, and Saint John on charity.[21] In the poem there are further allegorical triads of *tre donne*, whose identities are not always clear.[22] There are also such enigmatic feminine personages from the Old Testament as Rahab the harlot.[23]

But by far the most prominent of all the *tre donne* are the three Eternal Feminines—historical, and yet allegorical, and therefore theological—with whom this book deals: Beatrice as *donna mia*, the Church as *bella sposa*, and the Blessed Virgin Mary as *nostra regina*. All three appear in Canto XXIII of the *Paradiso*,[24] but they, and the complex interrelations among them, dominate the *Paradiso* from beginning to end.

---

[16] *Purg*.XXIX.121–129.

[17] *Par*.XX.127–129.

[18] They are *fede*, *speranza*, and *caritate* in Italian; *fides*, *spes*, and *charitas* in Latin. On the other hand, the Latin *amor* and its Italian cognate *amore*, in such passages as Canto XXVI of the *Paradiso* and of course in the closing line of the entire poem (*Par*.XXXIII.145), is masculine.

[19] *Par*.I.39.

[20] *Par*.XXIV.40.

[21] *Par*.XXIV–XXVI.

[22] For example, *Purg*.XXXI.130–138.

[23] *Par*.IX.112–126; see the interpretation of Bergin 1959, 23–24.

[24] Beatrice (*Par*.XXIII.34); the Church (*Par*.XXIII.19–20); Mary (*Par*. XXIII.73–74).

Each of the three is "a celestial and a terrestrial phenomenon."[25] Each has had a real history on earth before she appears in paradise; and the *poesia teologica*,[26] the theological significance of each, lies precisely in the subtle and dialectical counterpoint in her between the Eternal and the Feminine, between the historical and the allegorical. Dante's treatment of that counterpoint, however, is different for each of the three. Beatrice as Eternal Feminine is a real woman whom he has known only as she existed on earth but whom he now promotes (or sees God as having promoted) to a position in heaven, projecting for her an entire paradisiacal existence. Mary as Eternal Feminine is also a real woman, but one whom (by contrast with Beatrice) Dante has known only according to her existence in heaven, whose queen she is; his exposition is devoted to the connection between that heavenly existence and her relation with earth. And the Church as Eternal Feminine is a metaphor, whose roots are so deep and explicit in the language of the Bible itself and in the Catholic tradition that it is easy for Dante to escalate the metaphor into a reality for which such terms as "symbol" and "metaphor," if not also "allegory," have become altogether inadequate. For, as Erich Auerbach described the dialectic of earth and heaven, speaking about another triad who put in their appearance earlier than the *Paradiso*—a triad that also includes Beatrice, but that brackets Cato and Virgil with her, rather than the Church and Mary—"their appearance in the other world is a fulfillment of their appearance on earth, their earthly appearance a figure of their appearance in the other world."[27] Because of their prominence in the *Divine Comedy*, each of these three Eternal Feminines has, of course, received attention from the commentators and the scholars. The scholarly literature has also noted the relations among them, but only a few studies have put them into a larger context.[28]

---

[25] Guzzo 1959, 52–53.

[26] Chiavacci Leonardi 1963, 172–174.

[27] Auerbach 1953, 195.

[28] For example, Shapiro 1975.

"No single issue in the *Divine Comedy*," a distinguished student of Dante has observed, "has been more divisive and more persistently debated by Dante scholarship than that of allegory."[29] To readers who are acquainted with some of that Dante scholarship it will be evident that the analysis of Dante's method which occupies the remainder of this book, proceeding as it does on the basis of the history of biblical exegesis and of Christian doctrine during the patristic and medieval periods, does not accept a sharp distinction (as drawn, for example, by Auerbach) between the schema of *figura* and allegory. Auerbach justifies such a distinction on the grounds that "a figural schema permits both its poles—the figure and its fulfillment—to retain the characteristics of concrete historical reality, in contradistinction to what obtains with symbolic or allegorical personifications."[30] But what Francis Cornford said about the contrast between "allegory" and Platonic myth applies here as well: "An allegory, like a cypher, has a key; the *Pilgrim's Progress* can be retranslated into the terms of Bunyan's theology."[31] The *Divine Comedy* can likewise be translated into the terms of Dante's theology. For Augustinian *allegoria* (and Dantean theological allegory) does indeed, in Auerbach's phrase, retain the historical characteristics of each of these Eternal Feminines, even while it is pointing beyond them to their eternal meaning. Therefore, we shall continue to refer to "theological allegory."[32] As C. S. Lewis once noted, "allegory consists in giving an imagined body to the immaterial; but if, in each case, Catholicism claims already to have given it a material body, then the allegorist's symbol will naturally resemble that material body."[33]

Beryl Smalley has observed in her masterful book, *The Study of the Bible in the Middle Ages*, that "the allegorical

[29]Mazzotta 1979, 227.

[30]Auerbach 1953, 195.

[31]Cornford 1957, 32.

[32]Pépin 1970 has clarified this issue for the study of Dante in the context of medieval biblical exegesis. He has summarized his views in *Enc.Dant.* 1:151–165.

[33]Lewis 1951, 322.

method captivated the Latin world, and could be used more freely since it had ceased to be dangerous.... The Latin Fathers made their allegories conform to orthodox theology.... St. Jerome left a tradition on one hand of fanciful spiritual, on the other of scholarly literal interpretation.... St. Augustine welded together these different elements into a philosophy of Bible study.... St. Jerome gave the medieval scholar his text and his learned apparatus; St. Augustine told him what his aim should be."[34] Both the "learned apparatus" and the "allegorical method" seem to have held a special fascination for Dante, who gave himself ample opportunity in the *Divine Comedy* to use both. The learned apparatus comes to evidence in his allusions and etymologies, in his historical-biographical erudition, and in his geographical and astronomical lore. The allegorical method, which is our primary interest here, expresses itself in the *Divine Comedy*, as it does in other medieval literary works, in two ways that are distinct, even though they are also often interwoven: through an allegorical interpretation of Scripture and through the creation of allegories, including especially theological allegories, in the text. A prime example of the first is the allegorical interpretation of the Song of Solomon, which was, as Dom Leclercq has observed on the basis of his lifelong study of these texts, "the book which was most read, and most frequently commented in the medieval cloister."[35] A particularly striking instance of allusion to the Song of Songs is the tercet in Canto X:

> Then, like a clock that calls us at the hour
> in which the Bride of God, on waking, sings
> matins to her Bridegroom, encouraging
> His love....[36]

But the allegorical exegesis of the Song is reflected in other passages of the *Paradiso* as well. As Chapter 4, "The Church as

---

[34] Smalley 1964, 20–23.
[35] Leclercq 1961, 90.
[36] *Par.* X.139–141.

*Bella Sposa*," will describe at some length, however, the biblical allegory of Christ and the Church moves almost imperceptibly into a literary and theological allegory of Dante's own, in which he uses the allegory of Bride and Bridegroom to convey a lesson about the Church, so otherworldly and yet so worldly. The theological allegory of "Mary as *Nostra Regina*," expounded in Chapter 5, is less explicitly grounded in Scripture than is that in Chapter 4, although, as a recent study has pointed out, "this subject [the Coronation of Mary] was treated widely in the medieval exegetical literature."[37] And, of course, the allegory of "Beatrice as *Donna Mia*," the theme of chapter 3, is even less scriptural than that. Nevertheless, these other two theological allegories of Eternal Feminines do perform an analogous function in the *Paradiso*, and the three deserve to be considered together.

----

[37] Fiero et al. 1989, 115.

# ONE

# The Otherworldly World of the *Paradiso*

As even the cursory examination of a bibliography on Dante or of a library card catalog will suggest, the third and final *cantica* of the *Divine Comedy* by Dante Alighieri, the *Paradiso*, has, for whatever reason, received considerably less attention than the other two. On the other hand, the *Inferno* is the most prominent—perhaps because it is the first, or possibly because it is the most vividly dramatic, or probably because it is existentially the most accessible to the reader. Yet the *Paradiso* is in many ways the cantica of most interest to the history of Christian theology and dogma. Thomas Bergin has trenchantly summarized its doctrinal import: "For Dante, paradise was clearly the place where one learned things, so that there is more overt didactic matter in the *Paradiso* than in the other *cantiche*. It is not entirely fanciful to find significance in the fact that the word '*dottrina*' occurs twice in the *Inferno*, four times in the *Purgatorio*, and six times in the *Paradiso*; nor to note that the *Inferno* begins with a straightforward narrative statement, the *Purgatorio* with a metaphor, and the *Paradiso* with a statement of dogma. And with dogma, clearly and forcefully put, the *Paradiso* is replete."[1] It is, then, with that cantica that the present study in the history of theology deals—surely an ambitious undertaking, if not indeed a presumptuous one.

---

[1] Bergin 1965, 274.

For a scholar, there is some consolation to be derived from the awareness that any presumption involved in this assignment falls far short of that entailed by the composition of a work of literature whose author dares to assert, already in its second sentence and its second tercet:

> I was within the heaven that receives
> more of His light; and I saw things that he
> who from that height descends, forgets or can
> not speak.[2]

In those lines the poet is echoing, no doubt consciously,[3] the words of another visionary. As most interpreters ancient and modern would agree, the apostle Paul was speaking about himself when he wrote to the Corinthians: "I will come to visions and revelations of the Lord. I knew a man in Christ above fourteen years ago (whether in the body, I cannot tell; or whether out of the body, I cannot tell: God knoweth); such an one caught up to the third heaven. And I knew such a man (whether in the body, I cannot tell; or whether out of the body, I cannot tell: God knoweth); how that he was caught up into paradise, and heard unspeakable words, which it is not lawful for a man to utter."[4] (Of course, although Saint Paul, at any rate most of the time, leaves such "unspeakable words [ἄρρητα ῥήματα]" unspoken, Dante does go on for the next thirty-three cantos of the *Paradiso* to describe, from among the things he saw, at least all those which he that descended from the light does have both the knowledge and the power to tell again.) It is, fortunately, not the task of the scholar to reenact, or to participate in, the visions of an ancient seer—be it Saint Paul in the third heaven or Saint John the Divine in the Apocalypse, or Virgil in hell and purgatory, or Dante in paradise—but only to give a faithful account of the text of the

---

[2]*Par.*I.4–6.
[3]Mazzeo 1958, 84–110.
[4]2 Cor. 12:1–4.

*Paradiso* and to put it into context, specifically its broader historical context in the theology and piety of the late Middle Ages, or what we are calling in this chapter "the otherworldly world of the *Paradiso.*" The *Paradiso* belongs to the late Middle Ages first of all, of course, because that is when its author lived.[5] Dante Alighieri was born in Florence sometime between 21 May and 21 June[6] in 1265—thus, exactly fifty years after the greatest church council of the Middle Ages, the Fourth Lateran held in 1215. Dante's birth came just one year after Roger Bacon's composition of the *De Computo Naturali* [On Natural Computation], one year after Thomas Aquinas's *Summa contra Gentiles*, and two years after the founding of Balliol College. And he died in exile, at Ravenna, in 1321, nineteen years before the birth of Geoffrey Chaucer. Thus, it was during Dante's lifetime that Pope Boniface VIII, indelibly pictured in Canto XXVII of the *Inferno*[7] (as well as in other passages, though he is named only once),[8] ascended the throne of Saint Peter in 1294, and during his lifetime that Pope Clement V moved the papacy from Rome to Avignon. John Wycliffe, moreover, was born only seven years after Dante died. In anyone's chronology, therefore, Dante belongs to the Middle Ages, much as he is connected also to the Renaissance.[9]

Yet it is in far more than a literal chronological sense that Dante's *Divine Comedy*, and specifically the *Paradiso*, belongs

---

[5]Vossler 1929 continues to be an indispensable introduction to the entire world of Dante.

[6]That is the conclusion most scholars draw from Dante's words (*Par.*XXII.111–120) about "the sign that follows Taurus," that is to say, Gemini, the "constellation steeped in mighty force [*gran virtù*]," as his "fated point of entry," to which all of his genius looks as its source.

[7]*Inf.*XXVII.67–129.

[8]*Inf.*XIX.53.

[9]On this latter connection, it is instructive to note that throughout *The Civilization of the Renaissance in Italy* Jacob Burckhardt celebrated Dante as the embodiment of his major themes. What he said in chapter 3 of Part II could have been said of each part: "Here, again, as in all essential points, the first witness to be called is Dante" (Burckhardt 1958, 1:151).

to the Middle Ages. As Thomas Bergin has said, the images of the poem "cover all kinds of human activities, giving us such a richness of objective correlatives as to bring into the great 'hall of the *Comedy*' all forms and features of the medieval world." At the same time, Bergin observes, "Dante's great work is concerned with matters not of this world; his subject is the afterlife, his pilgrimage takes him into realms which cannot be charted on physical maps, and his interests are in things eternal and not temporal."[10] For that *is* the world of the *Divine Comedy*, even and especially of the *Paradiso*: the otherworldly world view of Western Christendom at the end of the thirteenth and the beginning of the fourteenth century. "World view" here does refer, of course, to cosmology, and from time to time we shall have occasion to examine Dante's universe. But "world view," *Weltanschauung*, includes as well the vision of life and of reality with which the entire poem is suffused. For the *Paradiso*, that means first and foremost a view of this world in the light of the world to come, of *Terra* in the light of *Inferno* and *Purgatorio* and *Paradiso*, of time in the light of eternity, *sub specie aeternitatis*. To read the poem intelligently, it is not necessary to share, but it is necessary to try to imagine and thus to understand, a conception of reality in which the very definition of being, the "is-ness" of what "is," has been set by the Ultimate Reality and Ultimate Being that is God. Thus when Dante, addressing the apostle Peter, paraphrases the Nicene Creed and quotes its opening words, "Io credo in uno Dio," he declares:

> For this belief I have not only proofs
> both physical and metaphysical;
> I also have the truth that here rains down
> through Moses

and others of the Old and the New Testament.[11] As his earlier reference to "your dear brother," the apostle Paul, makes

---

[10]Bergin 1965, 286 and 1.
[11]*Par.*XXIV.130–141.

clear, Dante is referring to the celebrated definition of faith in the Epistle to the Hebrews (regarded as having been written by Paul): "Faith is the substance of things hoped for, the evidence of things not seen."[12] The "proofs both physical and metaphysical" should probably be taken as more or less equivalent to the familiar "five ways" of proving the existence of God set down by Saint Thomas Aquinas on almost the first page of the *Summa*.[13] But the reference to "Moses" is an echo of the saying of God quoted by Thomas in that discussion and addressed to Moses from the burning bush, "I am that I am,"[14] which Dante, together with the consensus of thinkers Jewish and Christian, takes to mean that God is Being itself, while all other "being," whether visible or invisible, angelic or inanimate, as the same Creed affirms, is the creation of that God and hence possesses its being derivatively and dependently.

The "world of the *Paradiso*," however, must mean even more specifically what cannot be called anything except its "otherworldly world." As the striking epigram of Shirley Jackson Case put it, "The sky hung low in the ancient world,"[15] and it continued to do so in Dante's medieval world. For not only does Dante present the Being of God as the Ultimate Reality in relation to which all other "being" has a secondary reality, thus providing what Arthur Lovejoy has called "a fairly unequivocal expression of the principle of plenitude";[16] but the primacy of the divine reality of God the Creator is, in a mysterious fashion, shared with all the creaturely dwellers of paradise as well, transforming their very existence into another order of being. That applies in a special way to the angels, but perhaps the most dramatic (and almost certainly the most enigmatic) case of such transformation is Beatrice. Whatever may be the status of "the quest of the historical Beatrice," she is, here in the *Paradiso* and above all in its closing cantos,

---

[12] *Par*.XXIV.61–66, quoting Heb. 11:1.
[13] *S.T.*I.2.3.
[14] Exod. 3:14.
[15] Case 1946, 1.
[16] Lovejoy 1936, 68–69.

beyond time and space and almost (though not quite) beyond creatureliness itself. "If that which has been said of her so far," Dante summarizes,

> were all contained within a single praise [*in una loda*],
> it would be too scant to serve me now.
> The loveliness I saw surpassed not only
> our human measure—and I think that, surely,
> only its Maker can enjoy it fully.[17]

Therefore, the intuition of Gertrud Bäumer is correct when she relates Dante to the closing lines of Goethe's *Faust*.[18] Its final line, "*Das Ewig-Weibliche zieht uns hinan* [The Eternal Feminine draws us above]," unforgettably set to music by Gustav Mahler in his Eighth Symphony, does echo Dante's apotheosis of Beatrice; and it was therefore natural for it to provide the title for this book. In present-day English usage, however, the term "otherworldly" usually means "spectral" (or "spooky") and therefore suggests something "unreal," while in the *Paradiso* it is precisely the "otherworldliness" that is "really real." As A. Bartlett Giamatti put it, "all the landscapes of Hell and Purgatory are either defective or incomplete versions of the terrestrial paradise. But the terrestrial paradise is itself only an image of the celestial paradise. The garden of Eden simply reflects the City of God."[19]

At the same time, this "otherworldliness" of the *Paradiso* must not be taken to mean that Dante's consideration of this world of time and space, the world of politics and of human history, is confined to the *Inferno* and the *Purgatorio*, in both of which (as even the most casual reader can recognize) it is so prominent. On the contrary, it is possible to argue that in those first two cantiche Dante could treat politics and history as incisively and as severely as he did for the very reason that

---

[17] *Par*.XXX.16–21.
[18] Bäumer 1949, 149; also Newman 1987, 262.
[19] Giamatti 1966, 116.

even then he had his eye on a rule of measurement beyond the here and now. That becomes strikingly evident, for example, in the portrait of the emperor Justinian which occupies all of Canto VI of the *Paradiso*, with a prelude at the conclusion of Canto V and a curious liturgical cadenza (employing a mixture of Latin and quasi-Hebrew words) in the opening three lines of Canto VII.[20] Justinian introduces himself to the poet as the lawgiver of Rome, the one

> who, through the will of the Primal Love I feel,
> removed the vain and needless from the laws.[21]

According to this definition of jurisprudence, what the law expresses is not the harsh reality of moral ambiguity in the world of politics (an ambiguity that Dante knew well from his own Florentine experience, and about which he repeatedly speaks with great bitterness in the *Divine Comedy*), but the will and purpose of the *primo Amor*, which embodies itself in natural and positive law, even though, as in the empyrean,

> where God governs with no mediator [*sanza mezzo*],
> no thing depends upon the laws of nature,[22]

much less upon the positive legislation of human societies. Justinian's introduction is followed by a remarkable survey of the history of Rome, in which one Caesar after another passes in review, from the original Caesar, Julius, to the Holy Roman Emperor Charlemagne. "Caesar I was and am Justinian [*Cesare fui e son Iustiniano*]," the emperor declares,[23] setting the criterion of law and justice as an absolute standard by which to measure all his predecessors—and all his successors as well, up to and including the political parties and partisans of

---

[20]*Enc.Dant.*3:231–233.
[21]*Par.*VI.10–12.
[22]*Par.*XXX.122–123.
[23]*Par.*VI.10.

Dante's own time in the empire. "Let Ghibellines," the emperor Justinian asserts as, speaking from the sixth century, he addresses himself to the problems of the fourteenth,

> pursue their undertakings
> beneath another sign, for those who sever
> this sign and justice are bad followers.[24]

It is this medieval otherworldliness of the *Paradiso* that, far from having abstracted Dante out of the real world of politics and concrete choice, enables him to pass specific judgment on conditions in the empire past and present.

That applies a fortiori to his treatment of the Church, to which we shall be returning in greater detail but which is appropriate here as a prime illustration of the otherworldly world that is the context of the *Paradiso*. The century of the *Paradiso* is also the century of Boniface VIII and of the "Babylonian captivity" of the Church under the Avignon papacy and, on the other hand, the century of John Wycliffe at Oxford and then (beginning in the fourteenth century but continuing into the fifteenth) of Jan Hus in Prague. Dante was caught up passionately in the agitation for the reform of the Church, of its hierarchy, and of the papacy itself. This is evident from Dante's other writings, above all from the *De Monarchia*, which it is a mistake to read only as a treatise on secular politics, as though there were no difference between Dante's *De Monarchia* and the *Defensor Pacis* of Marsilius of Padua; for, as a leading student of Marsilius has pointed out, "even Dante, despite his dedication of the 'temporal monarchy' to intellectual activity, also finally apportions the papal function to caring for man's incorruptible soul, and the temporal imperial function to man's corruptible body."[25] The passage cited earlier from the *Inferno* indicates what Dante thought of Pope Boniface VIII. But all of that denunciation of corruption in the Church and in the

---

[24] *Par*.VI.103–105.
[25] Gewirth 1951, 100, n. 54.

papacy does not, as one might have expected, come to its crescendo in the hell or in the purgatory to which so many of the past occupants of the throne of Saint Peter have been consigned by Dante (and, presumably, by God), but here in heaven, where it is Saint Peter himself,

> that ancient father
> of Holy Church, into whose care the keys
> of this fair flower were consigned by Christ,[26]

who pronounces their judgment upon them—just as it is from the vantage point of heaven that its former inhabitant, "the first proud being [*'l primo superbo*]" who was "the highest of all creatures,"[27] Satan the fallen angel, must be judged. Beginning with an Italian metric version of the Latin Gloria Patri, Canto XXVII goes on to these stinging words from Peter, the Prince of the Apostles. Three times Saint Peter plaintively cries out "my place [*il luogo mio*]," just as, fulfilling Christ's grim prophecy, he had denied his Lord three times:[28]

> He who on earth usurps my place, my place,
> my place that in the sight of God's own Son
> is vacant now, has made my burial ground
> a sewer of blood, a sewer of stench, so that
> the perverse one who fell from Heaven, here
> above, can find contentment there below.[29]

Apparently, as the Church is viewed by none other than Saint Peter himself in the light of the other world, such a corrupt Church could provide a more comfortable domicile for Satan than it could—or, at any rate, than it should—for any legitimate successor of Peter.

The "otherworldly" criterion in the *Paradiso*'s treatment of

---

[26] *Par.*XXXII.124–126.
[27] *Par.*XIX.46–48.
[28] Matt.26:34, 69–75.
[29] *Par.*XXVII.22–27.

the Church and its reform makes itself visible also in the prominent role that the *Paradiso* assigns to monks and to monasticism. For, in the vocabulary of the Middle Ages, the monastic life was often called "the angelic life [*vita angelica*]." In the Gospel, Christ had said that "in the resurrection [human beings] neither marry, nor are given in marriage, but are as the angels of God in heaven."[30] Saint Gregory of Nyssa used the saying from the Gospel to argue that since "the resurrection promises us nothing else than the restoration of the fallen to their ancient state," virginity was characteristic of "the life before the transgression" of Adam and Eve, which for that reason was "a kind of angelic life."[31] On that basis, virginity and therefore monasticism had been referred to as "angelic" by Gregory's brother, the father of Eastern monasticism, Saint Basil of Caesarea, as well as by Saint John Chrysostom.[32] Perhaps from such Greek sources, Rufinus of Aquileia, who knew the Greek Christian authors well and translated some of them into Latin, spoke of monasticism as the *vita angelica*, as did other Latin writers.[33] And in the supplement to Part III of the *Summa Theologica* the term is explained this way: "Virginity is said to be an 'angelic life,' insofar as virgins imitate by grace what angels have by nature. For it is not owing to a virtue that angels abstain altogether from pleasures of the flesh, since they are incapable of such pleasures."[34] It seems plausible that "the bread of angels" of which Dante speaks in the *Paradiso*[35] refers to the wisdom of the angels who, because they did not fall from grace with their fellows,

> were modestly aware
> that they were ready for intelligence
> so vast, because of that Good which had made them.[36]

---

[30] Matt. 22:30.
[31] Gregory of Nyssa *On the Making of Man* xvii.2.
[32] Lampe 1961, 9; on "Chrysostom the metropolitan," see *Par*.XII.136–137.
[33] Blaise and Chirat 1954, 81.
[34] *S.T.*III, Sup.96.9. *ad* 1.
[35] For example, *Par*.II.11.
[36] *Par*.XXIX.58–60; see also the Epilogue below.

But the "angelic life" in the usage of his time is a way of speaking about monasticism, a usage that Dante does reflect here in the *Paradiso* when—alluding to the traditional distinction according to which "the cherubim have the excellence of knowledge and the seraphim the excellence of ardor" in their charity[37]—he says that Saint Dominic was "cherubic" whereas Saint Francis was "seraphic."[38]

Even without running a detailed and precise statistical analysis, moreover, it is striking to note how often monastic figures and monastic themes appear throughout the entire third cantica of the *Divine Comedy*.[39] For example, the words of Piccarda Donati in Canto III, "We have neglected vows,"[40] are followed by the poet's question at the end of Canto IV:

> I want to know if, in your eyes, one can
> amend for unkept vows with other acts.[41]

This is followed in turn by Beatrice's response about vows at the beginning of Canto V.[42] All of this carries echoes of the most extensive discussions of vows in medieval thought, which were addressed to monastic vows. Therefore, the interpreters who have detected a note of irony in Beatrice's explanation that "the Holy Church gives dispensations"[43] are probably correct. For a vow, in Beatrice's (and Dante's) view, is not merely an agreement between two human beings, even if one of them is a priest or prelate, but ultimately a sacred contract between creature and Creator. That vertical dimension is what makes the betrayal of a vow such a crime, as can be seen also in the various cases of marital infidelity, "the force

---

[37] *S.T.* I.108.5. *ad* 6.

[38] *Par.* XI.37–39.

[39] As Palgen 1940, 66–67, has noted, the only two souls who speak to Dante in the Heaven of Saturn are both monks, Saint Benedict and Saint Peter Damian.

[40] *Par.* III.56.

[41] *Par.* IV.136–137.

[42] *Par.* V.13–15.

[43] *Par.* V.35–36.

of Venus' poison,"[44] that appear in the *Inferno* and the *Purgatorio*. Here in the *Paradiso* the crime of betraying monastic vows evokes from the eleventh-century reformer of monasticism and of the Church, Saint Peter Damian, this lament:

> That cloister used to offer souls to Heaven,
> a fertile harvest, but it now is barren—
> as Heaven's punishment will soon make plain.[45]

For throughout the Middle Ages, as R. W. Southern has put it, "those who set themselves a standard higher than the ordinary looked to the monasteries for their examples,"[46] because the monasteries were the outposts of the other world here in this world, the models of authentic community, the seedbeds of holiness, and the sources of renewal. If they themselves became corrupt, as they did with such depressing regularity—

> The flesh of mortals yields so easily;
> on earth a good beginning does not run
> from when the oak is born until the acorn

is Dante's one-sentence lament[47]—the result was that not only the monks but everyone would suffer. In the familiar maxim of the Roman poet Juvenal, "*Sed quis custodiet ipsos custodes?* [But who is to guard the guards themselves?]"[48]

Or, in the complaint that Dante puts into the mouth of the sixth-century founder of Western monasticism, Saint Benedict of Nursia,

> my Rule is left
> to waste the paper it was written on.[49]

---

[44]*Purg*.XXV.132.

[45]*Par*.XXI.118–120; see the discussion of Dante's use of medieval legends about Peter Damian in Capetti 1906.

[46]Southern 1953, 158.

[47]*Par*.XXII.85–87.

[48]Juvenal *Satires* VI.347–348.

[49]*Par*.XXII.74–75.

But that complaint is voiced by one who is already in heaven, as Beatrice is obliged to remind Dante about himself.[50] Indeed, he is not only in heaven, but (as she also reminds him) Dante has, at the point of encountering Benedict, come very "near the final blessedness."[51] At that exalted position, moreover, Benedict speaks as "the largest and most radiant"[52] of the hundred pearls or "little spheres [*sperule*]" to which Beatrice directs Dante's gaze. With the kind of spiritual boasting of which the apostle Paul speaks,[53] Benedict describes the achievements of his monastic foundation on Monte Cassino, built on the site of a pagan temple: "Such abundant grace had brought me light," he says,

> that, from corrupted worship that seduced
> the world, I won away the nearby sites.[54]

In so doing, Benedict established a pattern that was to become an essential component of monastic life throughout the rest of Christian history, as over and over the monks in both East and West were to be the shock troops of the Catholic and Christian faith, in the vanguard of its march across the continents. It was for this reason, among others, that in the twentieth century Saint Benedict and Saints Cyril and Methodius, the apostles to the Slavs, have been designated co-patron saints of Europe. From Dante's celebration of monastic heroism and from his lament over monastic vice, it is clear that in Dante's eyes the history of monasticism since the age of Benedict contained some of the most glorious chapters of Christian heroism, and some of the most degenerate chapters of Christian betrayal. Yet it is undeniable that for Dante the monks were among the leading citizens of both the Church on earth and the Church in paradise.

---

[50]*Par*.XXII.7–8.
[51]*Par*.XXII.124.
[52]*Par*.XXII.28.
[53]2 Cor. 11:16–33.
[54]*Par*.XXII.43–45.

Despite the high praise for Saint Benedict, the father of Western monasticism, the pride of place among the monks in the *Paradiso* is reserved for another monk who was not a Benedictine but a Cistercian, the monastic reformer who was also a reformer of the Church, Saint Bernard of Clairvaux.[55] In the final three cantos, which may well be the most powerful hymn ever written in praise of the Blessed Virgin Mary, the speaker is Bernard the "holy elder [*santo sene*]."[56] He describes himself as "Mary's faithful Bernard [*suo fedel Bernardo*]."[57] As Masseron has suggested, that title applies to Dante as well as to Bernard.[58] In this closing scene Bernard has left

> the sweet
> place where eternal lot assigns [his] seat,[59]

in order to expound to Dante the historical typology of Eve the mother of humankind and Mary the Second Eve. The speeches about Mary that Dante places into the mouth of Bernard are in fact a compendium of his rich and varied works devoted to her praises. Other works of Bernard of Clairvaux, particularly his letters and his treatise *On Consideration*, written for his pupil Pope Eugenius III, were likewise a source upon which Dante and his fellow reformers of church and empire drew for their denunciation of the Church's corruption.[60] In addressing such an essay as *On Consideration* to the pope, Bernard had clearly risen above the corruption of his time to carry out the historic responsibility of the monks as the conscience of the medieval Church.[61]

---

[55] See the long footnote discussing the question "Why Saint Bernard?" in Rabuse 1972, 59–61.

[56] *Par*.XXXI.94.

[57] *Par*.XXXI.102.

[58] Masseron 1953, 71–143.

[59] *Par*.XXXII.101–102.

[60] *Ep*.X.28.

[61] Kennan 1967.

In Dante's own time it was neither the Benedictines nor the Cistercians, but the Franciscans and the Dominicans who had assumed much of the responsibility for the spiritual life of the Church—and who had, yet again, manifested the universal tendency to corruption through "their decadence, and sudden passion for the material goods their masters had taught them to abandon, [which] destroyed many of the spiritual gains made by Francis and Dominic, and reduced the Orders to a state little better than that of the Church their founders had begun to rebuild."[62] The founders of these two orders are the subject of Canto XI of the *Paradiso*:

> two princes, one
> on this side, one on that [*quinci e quindi*], as her [the Church's]
> guides[63]—

one of them, as noted earlier, "all seraphic in his ardor" and the other "the splendor of cherubic light on earth."[64] In his miniature biography of Francis, in which scholars have found a remarkably "symmetrical construction,"[65] Dante describes how Francis had, after an interval of "some eleven hundred years,"[66] restored the primitive Christian ideal of poverty when he took Lady Poverty as his spiritual bride. Although this bizarre act brought upon him the "scorn and wonder [*maraviglia*]"[67] of most of his contemporaries, he did manage to extract from Pope Innocent III the approval of the Rule of the Franciscans, or, as Dante calls it, "the first seal of his order."[68] What Dante then goes on to call "the final seal [*l'ultimo sigillo*]," which "his limbs bore for two years,"[69] came in the form of

---

[62] Needler 1969, 21.
[63] *Par*.XI.36.
[64] *Par*.XI.37–39.
[65] Santarelli 1969, 37.
[66] *Par*.XI.65.
[67] *Par*.XI.90.
[68] *Par*.XI.93.
[69] *Par*.XI.107–108.

the stigmata, the marks of the Passion of Christ on the body of Saint Francis. Francis was and still is a controversial figure, indeed a revolutionary one. The implications of his doctrine and practice of poverty came to be seen by many of his followers, particularly the Spiritual Franciscans, as a radical attack upon the institutional Church as such, earning for them the condemnation of the Church's leaders. Nevertheless at his death this "second Christ," as he came to be known, issued a *Testament* (now generally acknowledged to be genuine) to his Franciscan brethren, in which

> Francis commended his most precious lady,
> and he bade them to love her faithfully.[70]

The official biographer of Saint Francis and the most eminent theological mind of the Franciscan Order (at least until Duns Scotus, who was born in the same year as Dante, 1265) was Bonaventure, who speaks in Canto XII of the *Paradiso*.

But it is one of the most striking of the many transpositions in the entire *Divine Comedy*, as many readers have noted and as a Dominican scholar has recently explained in some detail, that Bonaventure speaks not about Saint Francis but about Saint Dominic, founder of the Order of Preachers, just as it is the Dominican Thomas Aquinas who speaks in such glowing terms about Francis, founder of the Order of Friars Minor.[71] Writing at a time when the rivalry between the two orders and the general state of the monastic life had become a scandal throughout Western Christendom,[72] Dante employs this device to remind his readers—and any Franciscans or Dominicans

---

[70] *Par.*XI.113–114. Although some interpreters have taken this "most precious lady" to be Poverty, the tenor of my argument here seems to point to the conclusion that she is the Catholic Church.

[71] Foster 1987, 229–249.

[72] On the state of monastic life and monastic reform in the later Middle Ages, see the helpful summary of Oakley 1979, 231–238.

who might be listening—that the two emphases, the "se-raphic" celebration of the supremacy of love associated with the Franciscans and the "cherubic" cultivation of wisdom and scholarship identified with the Dominicans, are by no means mutually exclusive, but in fact need each other to be rescued from exaggeration. They are like two wheels of the chariot of Holy Church,[73] both of them indispensable to her journey on this earthly pilgrimage to the otherworldly paradise. There-fore, after Aquinas has begun by pointing to Dominic as "our patriarch [*il nostro patriarca*],"[74] it is Bonaventure who takes over to draw a vivid portrait of Dominic as "the holy athlete," whose valiant efforts as a formidable champion in defense of the truth of the Catholic faith made him "kind to his own and harsh to enemies."[75] In Dominic, it was above all the power of his intellect[76] that equipped him for his special ministry:

> Then he, with both his learning and his zeal,
> and with his apostolic office, like
> a torrent hurtled from a mountain source,
> coursed, and his impetus, with greatest force,
> struck where the thickets of the heretics
> offered the most resistance.[77]

For an appreciation of "the otherworldly world of the *Para-diso*," the angelic world of cherubim and seraphim, the most important accent in Dante's treatment of the Franciscans and the Dominicans here in the *Paradiso* is his use of angelic metaphors for both: Francis "was all *seraphic* in his ardor," Dominic was endowed with "the splendor of *cherubic* light on earth"[78]—"on earth," because such light and such ardor were

---

[73]*Par*.XII.106–107.

[74]*Par*.XI.121.

[75]*Par*.XII.57.

[76]*Par*.XII.59: "la sua mente di viva virtute."

[77]*Par*.XII.97–102.

[78]*Par*.XI.37–39.

ordinarily part of the other world, but in these two "princes"
they had appeared in this world as well.

In this connection, however, it is necessary to examine one
suggestion of a possible historical connection of Dante with
the Franciscan Order, and to evaluate the suggestion of another historical connection between Dante and the Dominican
Order. It is clear from the presentation in Cantos XI and XII
just summarized that Dante was striving to be evenhanded in
his treatment of the two orders, of their two founders, and of
the shameful condition into which both of the orders had
fallen by his own time. Yet that evenhandedness, which was
apparently quite sincere and surely quite successful, must
not be permitted to obscure Dante's special personal bond
with the Franciscans. For like many late medieval figures—it
should be noted, for example, that in June 1496, upon arriving
in Cádiz, Spain, at the end of his second voyage, Christopher
Columbus "assumed the coarse brown habit of a Franciscan,
as evidence of repentance and humility"[79]—Dante had identified himself with Saint Francis. In Canto XVI of the *Inferno*
Dante says of himself: "Around my waist I had a cord as girdle
[*una corda intorno cinta*],"[80] a cord that Virgil borrows to use
as an enormous fishing line for catching the monster Geryon.[81]
Although this could be a purely symbolic allusion—for which
there is a parallel, for example, in the words of the *Purgatorio*
about Charles of Aragon as one who "wore the cord of every
virtue [*ogne valor portò cinta la corda*]"[82]—the Franciscan
cord did have a special significance for Dante, which some
scholars have seen expressed by his reference, here in the
description of Francis and his retinue in the *Paradiso*, to "the
lowly cord already round their waists."[83] The reference to

---

[79] Morison 1955, 102.
[80] *Inf.*XVI.106.
[81] See the review of recent critical scholarship on this passage in D'Amato
1972.
[82] *Purg.*VII.114, apparently a reference to Isa. 11:5.
[83] *Par.*XI.85–87.

the "cord" in Canto XVI of the *Inferno* has given rise to the
theory that Dante had once, as a young man, briefly joined the
Franciscan Order.[84] John D. Sinclair thinks it "may well be
true,"[85] while Charles S. Singleton insists that "these specula-
tions are without documentary evidence" and that "it is in no
way certain that D[ante] ever joined the Order, even as a ter-
tiary."[86] Whatever may be the truth of such reports about
Dante's early life, it does seem certain that when he died on
the night of 13 September 1321, after a journey to Venice, he
was buried at Ravenna in a small chapel near San Piero Mag-
giore (which is now, appropriately enough, called San Francesco)—and that he was "buried with honors, and in the
costume of the Franciscan order."[87]

On the other hand, the intellectual content of the *Divine
Comedy* has often been identified (in perhaps too hasty and
facile a conclusion on the basis of evidence that is at best tenu-
ous) not with the Franciscans at all, but with the Dominicans
and specifically with Saint Thomas Aquinas. This issue was
brought to the fore in the book *Dante le théologien*, published
in 1935 by the Dominican scholar and distinguished editor of
the *Commentary on the Sentences* of Thomas Aquinas, Pierre
Mandonnet, who is perhaps best known to students of the history of philosophy for his pioneering research on Siger of Brabant and Latin Averroist philosophy.[88] The most important
response to Mandonnet's thesis is that of Etienne Gilson, whom
many would regard as the most eminent historian of medieval
thought in the past hundred years.[89] In addition to many inci-
sive comments on the standing issues of Dante interpretation,
above all on the tangled problem of whether Beatrice has

---

[84] On the entire question of Dante and the Franciscans, see the studies of
Needler 1969, Santarelli 1969, and Foster 1987.

[85] Sinclair 1961, 1:213.

[86] Singleton in Toynbee 1965, 48.

[87] Bergin 1965, 44.

[88] Mandonnet 1935.

[89] Gilson 1949.

become more than human by the time Dante gets to the final cantos of the *Paradiso*, Gilson reviews the alleged dependence of Dante on Thomas in a section entitled "Dante's Thomism."[90] And despite his own standing as a Thomist scholar and despite the prominent place occupied by Saint Thomas in the *Paradiso*,[91] Gilson concludes that it is a mistake to read Dante as a partisan and disciple of Thomas in any but the most general sense.

He must rather be seen as a disciple of Saint Augustine—which is, after all, how Thomas also saw himself even when he was criticizing Augustine.[92] Many of the phrases and tropes that a student of Aquinas seems to recognize as Thomistic upon reading the *Divine Comedy* are in fact Augustinian.[93] Thomas Aquinas and Dante Alighieri were drawing upon a common source, who was likewise the source for most of medieval theology, and for much if not most of medieval philosophy as well. It is rather curious, then, that Augustine himself occupies a relatively small place in the *Comedy*.[94] He appears together with Saint Francis and Saint Benedict in the Tenth Heaven,[95] but he does not function as one of the dramatis personae in the way that Thomas and Bonaventure and, above all, Bernard of Clairvaux do; nor does the narrative of his life story receive any special place in the poem. Yet that very obscurity can be taken to mean that the presence and influence of Augustine are so pervasive throughout the *Purgatorio*, especially throughout the *Paradiso*, that he does not have to be one of the characters in the play, since he has provided so many of its lines—including what may well be the most familiar line in the entire work, the words of Piccarda Donati, "And in His will

---

[90] Gilson 1949, 226–242.
[91] *Par*.X.82–138. XI.16–XII.2, XII.110–111, 141, XIII.32–XIV.8.
[92] Gilson 1926.
[93] Mazzotta 1979, 147–191.
[94] *Enc.Dant*.1:80–82.
[95] *Par*.XXXII.35.

there is our peace [*E 'n la sua volontade è nostra pace*],"[96] words that seem to be an unmistakable echo of the words of Augustine in the *Confessions*, "In Thy good will is our peace."[97] Similar parallels abound throughout the *Divine Comedy*, above all perhaps in the *Paradiso*. All of these Augustinian, medieval, and "otherworldly" qualities of the world of the *Paradiso* come together in its employment of allegory, especially of theological allegory.

---

[96] *Par*.III.85.
[97] Augustine *Confessions* XIII.ix.10.

# TWO

# Lady Philosophy as
# *Nutrix* and *Magistra*

WHEN his Lady Beatrice died, Dante tells us in the *Convivio*,
it was to Boethius's *Consolation of Philosophy* that he turned
for solace.[1] As Edward Gibbon said, "the *Consolation of Philosophy* [is] a golden volume not unworthy of the leisure of
Plato or Tully [Cicero]"[2]—and not unworthy either of the grief
of Dante Alighieri, who describes what it meant to him:

> I remained so overwhelmed with grief that no comfort availed
> me. However, after some time, my mind, which was striving to
> regain its health, resolved (since neither mine own nor others'
> consolation was of any avail) to have recourse to the plan which
> a certain other disconsolate one had adopted for his consola-
> tion. And I set myself to read that book of Boethius, whose
> contents are known but to few, wherewith, when a prisoner and
> in exile, he had consoled himself.... And as it befalls that a man
> who is in search of silver sometimes, not without divine ordi-
> nance, finds gold beyond his expectations, so I, who sought for
> consolation, found not only healing for my grief, but instruc-
> tion [*non solamente alle mie lagrime rimedio, ma vocaboli
> d'autori e di scienze e di libri*].[3]

For "healing [*rimedio*]" and "instruction [*scienze*]" were the
very forms of "consolation" that Philosophia, as *nutrix* and as

---

[1] See the summary discussion, *Enc.Dant.* 1:654–658.
[2] Gibbon 1896–1900, 4:170, 200–201.
[3] *Conv.*II.13.

*magistra*, brought to Boethius. Living and writing (and eventually dying) in exile, where he came to

> know the bitter taste
> of others' bread, how salt it is, and know
> how hard a path it is for one who goes
> descending and ascending others' stairs,[4]

Dante is clearly affirming his kinship with Boethius, who in the *Consolation* speaks of his own *exilium*,[5] when he has Thomas Aquinas describe Boethius, though without even having to name him, in the *Paradiso*:

> Within that light,
> because he saw the Greatest Good, rejoices
> the blessed soul who makes the world's deceit
> most plain to all who hear him carefully.
> The flesh from which his soul was banished lies
> below, within Cieldauro, and he came
> from martyrdom and exile to this peace
> [*da martiro*
> *e da essilio venne a questa pace*].[6]

These words are echoed almost verbatim by Dante's ancestor, Cacciaguida, speaking about himself in a later canto of the *Paradiso*: "From martyrdom I came unto this peace."[7] They also went on to become the epitaph selected by William James for his sister Alice.[8]

There are other echoes of Boethius in Dante.[9] For example, he makes use of Boethius in each book of the *Convivio*.[10] One

---

[4]*Par.*XVII.55–60.

[5]*Cons.*II.pr.4.17.

[6]*Par.*X.124–129.

[7]*Par.*XV.148.

[8]Strouse 1980, 317; I am indebted for this information to my colleague, R.W.B. Lewis.

[9]Murari 1905, 377–403, suggests many of these, some nearly definite and others more far-fetched.

[10]*Conv.*I.2; II.8; III.1; IV.12–13.

such echo in the *Paradiso* has recently been noted by Peter Dronke. Just before the description of Boethius quoted above, Dante has Thomas Aquinas, having spoken of Orosius as "that champion of the Christian centuries" whose work was of assistance to Augustine in writing the *City of God*, continue:

> Now, if your mind's eye, following my praising,
> was drawn from light to light. . . . [11]

In the final book of the *Consolation*, Boethius observes that "we see many things with our eyes while they are in doing [*dum fiunt*]." [12] But then he goes on:

> Sense, imagination, reason and understanding do diversely behold a man. . . . The eye of the understanding [*intellegentiae oculus*] is higher yet. For surpassing the compass of the whole world it beholdeth with the clear eye of the mind [*pura mentis acie*] that simple form in itself. [13]

As Dronke suggests, "it is this insight that leads Boethius to his individual solution of the last and greatest problem in his work—the relation of eternity, divine providence, and human freedom," [14] and this insight for which Dante quotes him by speaking of the "mind's eye." Yet in most such attempts to assess the "influence" of Boethius or of anyone else on Dante, it is probably well to heed the warning of Howard Patch, the author of a study specifically dealing with this issue and entitled *The Tradition of Boethius*, who notes that "when [the ideas of Boethius] reappear in Dante's *Divine Comedy* it is hard to tell from what source they really came," [15] whether directly from Boethius or from any of several alternative authors, some but by no means all of whom were in turn de-

---

[11] *Par.*X.121–122.
[12] *Cons.*V.pr.4.15.
[13] *Cons.*V.pr.4.27–30.
[14] Dronke 1988, 97.
[15] Patch 1935, 33.

pendent on Boethius. For instance, when Dante speaks in the *Paradiso* of "sweet medicine [*soave medicina*]," [16] that may be, but it does not necessarily have to be, an allusion to the medical imagery that pervades the *Consolation*. Nevertheless, Helen Barrett has suggested one parallel between two passages in Boethius and in Dante that does seem quite plausible. [17] In Book II of the *Consolation*, addressing Lady Philosophy as *virtutum omnium nutrix*, Boethius declares: "This it is that which vexeth me most, when I remember it. For in all adversity of fortune it is the most unhappy kind of misfortune to have been happy [*infelicissimum est genus infortunii fuisse felicem*]." [18] Those words of Boethius do come to mind in the touching story of Paolo and Francesca in Canto V of the *Inferno*, when Francesca says to Dante:

> There is no greater sorrow
> than thinking back upon a happy time
> in misery—and this your teacher knows, [19]

the *tuo dottore* to whom Francesca is alluding being quite possibly Boethius (although this is a title that he has been using especially for Virgil). [20]

Like the Christian author of the Book of Revelation around the end of the first century and the Christian author of the *Divine Comedy* in the fourteenth century, the Christian author of the *Consolation of Philosophy* near the beginning of the sixth century opens his account with a vision. The Seer of the Apocalypse beholds

> . . . one like unto the Son of Man, clothed with a garment down to the foot, and girt about the paps with a golden girdle. His head and his hairs were white like wool, as white as snow; and

---

[16] *Par.*XX.141.
[17] Barrett 1940, 84.
[18] *Cons.*II.pr.4.1–2.
[19] *Inf.*V.121–123.
[20] *Inf.*V.70, XVI.13; *Purg.*XXI.22, XXI.131, XXIV.143.

his eyes were as a flame of fire; and his feet like unto fine brass, as if they burned in a furnace; and his voice as the sound of many waters. And he had in his right hand seven stars: and out of his mouth went a sharp two-edged sword: and his countenance was as the sun shineth in his strength.[21]

But Boethius in his allegorical vision—and Dante in his—sees something else, or rather someone other than the Son of Man:

> Methought I saw a *woman* stand above my head, having a grave countenance, glistening clear eye, and of quicker sight than commonly Nature doth afford; her color fresh and bespeaking unabated vigor, and yet discovering so many years that she could not at all be thought to belong to our times. . . . Sometimes she seemed to touch the heavens with her head, and if she lifted it up to the highest, she pierced the very heavens, so that she could not be seen by the beholders.[22]

The name of the woman is *Philosophia*, Lady Philosophy, and the *Consolation* consists of a dialogue between her and Boethius. Thus the genitive *Philosophiae* in the title of the work is a subjective genitive, meaning that she is the subject who does the consoling.

Philosophia is a woman: she is, in the phrase of Book I, "our Woman Leader [*nostra dux*]."[23] In the allegorical vision of Boethius she is identified as a woman by something that goes well beyond the kind of metaphor that speaks about God as the heavenly king riding in his chariot,[24] or about the Good as "the helm and rudder by which the frame of the world is kept steadfast and uncorrupted."[25] She is a woman, moreover, not only because of the grammatical accident (if that is what grammatical gender is) that the noun happens to be a first-

---

[21] Rev. 1:13–16.
[22] *Cons*.I.pr.1.1–2.
[23] *Cons*.I.pr.3.13.
[24] *Cons*.IV.m.1.219–222.
[25] *Cons*.III.pr.12.14.

declension feminine in Latin, as, for example, the grammatical gender of *voluptas* makes it possible for Boethius to speak of pleasure as a woman.[26] But in the case of Philosophia such a way of speaking has a special appropriateness, because the kinds of consolation she brings to Boethius are specifically "feminine"—in the sense in which Boethius could be expected to have understood that concept. For much, though probably not all, of the consoling can be subsumed under one of two heads, both of which are character traits and activities that he assigns to Philosophia specifically as a woman: she is *nutrix* and at the same time she is *magistra*, a nurse and a teacher. In Book II he calls her "nurse of all virtues [*virtutum omnium nutrix*],"[27] in Book I "teacher of all virtues [*omnium magistra virtutum*]."[28] Those two roles are represented by the two Greek letters on her garments when she appeared to the author: "In the lower part of them was placed the Greek letter Π, and in the upper Θ, and betwixt the two letters, in the manner of stairs, there were certain degrees made, by which there was a passage from the lower to the higher letter."[29] As Boethius himself explains elsewhere, the lower pi stands for "practical [πρακτική]" philosophy, and the upper theta for "speculative [θεωρητική]" philosophy;[30] but these two branches of philosophy also correspond, respectively, to Philosophia as *nutrix* and Philosophia as *magistra*. The close connection between the two, moreover, is according to the *Consolation* a fundamental presupposition of the teaching of Plato, who had been taught by Philosophia herself that "commonwealths would be blessed if they should be ruled by philosophers or if their rulers should happen to have studied philosophy,"[31] in other words, if the practical good sense of

---

[26] *Cons.*III.m.7.1–6.

[27] *Cons.*II.pr.4.1.

[28] *Cons.*I.pr.3.3.

[29] *Cons.*I.pr.1.4.

[30] Boethius *Dialogue on Porphyry* 1, as cited in all the editions here *ad locum*.

[31] *Cons.*I.pr.4.5.

Lady Philosophy as *nutrix* and the theoretical speculation of Lady Philosophy as *magistra* could coincide. This is the combination that Lady Philosophy has inculcated in Boethius when she "framed my conversation and the manner of my whole life according to the pattern of the celestial order,"[32] basing practical philosophy on theoretical philosophy. And the same combination is what she tries here to restore to one who needs both a nurse and a teacher, because he is suffering from "lethargy, the common disease of deceived minds."[33]

It is Philosophia's intent throughout the *Consolation* to convince Boethius, as the conclusion states, that (at the practical level symbolized by the pi on her garment) "it is not in vain [to] put our hope in God or pray to Him," because (at the speculative level symbolized by the theta on her garment) "there remaineth also a beholder of all things which is God."[34] This she does both as *nutrix* and as *magistra*. The Latin word *nutrix*, translated here as "nurse," refers in the first instance, both in classical usage and in the language of Boethius, to "nurse" in the sense of "nourisher"; but as the parallel verb *nutrire* is used in Latin also for "healing," it does not seem to be doing violence to the *Consolation* to extend the meaning of *nutrix* as well to that function, which comes closer to our English usage of the word "nurse" today than, strictly speaking, *nutrix* itself does.[35] Further justification for such an extension of meaning is suggested also by such statements of Lady Philosophy as this: "We have the greatest nourisher of thy health [*Habemus maximum tuae fomitem salutis*]."[36] For the loss of self-knowledge to which Philosophia as *magistra* points involves as well a need for healing to which Philosophia as *nutrix* addresses herself: "Now I know," she says to him near the end of Book I, "the cause, or the chief cause, of your sickness. You have forgotten what you are. Now therefore I have

[32]*Cons*.I.pr.4.4.
[33]*Cons*.I.pr.2.5.
[34]*Cons*.V.pr.6.45–46.
[35]*OED* 7–I:265–266.
[36]*Cons*.I.pr.6.20.

found out to the full the manner of your sickness, and how to attempt the restoring of your health."[37]

That imagery also plays a prominent part throughout the *Consolation* of Boethius, but especially in the earlier books, where Lady Philosophy takes the role of diagnostician.[38] She needs to "be rightly informed of the causes and condition of thy disease."[39] For, as she tells Boethius, "If thou expectest to be cured, thou must discover thy wound [*vulnus*]."[40] Only after finding out "the nature of the disease" will it be possible to prescribe "the manner of recovery."[41] As "a physician who knoweth the manner and temper both of health and sickness,"[42] she must be the one who probes to find the underlying and hidden sources of what afflicts him. He has made a lifetime study of investigating the "various causes" of what happens in nature.[43] But in his present state he cannot by himself identify within himself the real causes of sickness and death.[44] Finding him in his cell unable to communicate with her or perhaps even to recognize her, "she laid her hand upon [Boethius's] breast, saying: 'There is no danger; he is in a lethargy, the common disease of deceived minds.' "[45] A little later she returns to this diagnosis, reminding him that she has recognized how, "as by the breach of a fortress, the sickness of perturbations hath entered into thy mind."[46] It is, for example, "the weakness of the beholders' eyes" that often attributes a beautiful appearance to people like Alcibiades, when they are in fact "most foul and ugly."[47] But sometimes the disease goes far beyond mere "infirmity." That would be far too weak a

<hr />

[37] *Cons.*I.pr.6.17.
[38] Wolf 1964.
[39] *Cons.*II.pr.1.2.
[40] *Cons.*I.pr.4.1.
[41] *Cons.*I.pr.6.17.
[42] *Cons.*IV.pr.6.27–28.
[43] *Cons.*I.m.2.23.
[44] *Cons.*I.pr.6.19.
[45] *Cons.*I.pr.2.5.
[46] *Cons.*I.pr.6.9.
[47] *Cons.*III.pr.8.10.

word for "the furious rage of wicked Nero's spite."[48] His "rage and luxury [*luxuria saeviens*]" became a cautionary tale for anyone who would pursue worldly honor.[49] While Lady Philosophy is carrying out this diagnosis of Boethius and before she is in a position to prescribe and supply the remedies of his disease, she provides him with "certain fomentations to assuage thy grief, which as yet resisteth all cure."[50]

Part of the diagnosis of Lady Philosophy as *nutrix* is the identification of the disease of adhering to various false female deities and semi-deities. The dialogue does refers more than once to mother deities and to goddesses,[51] but more pertinent are the very first words that Philosophia utters, a scathing attack on the Muses of poetry, to whom Boethius has turned for consolation and who are "dictating words to accompany my tears." " 'Who,' " she demands, 'has allowed these hysterical sluts to approach this sick man's bedside?' " They are not authentic Muses: "Sirens is a better name for you and your deadly enticements: be gone, and leave him for my own Muses to heal and cure!"[52] As Anna Crabbe has said, "this stately lady's reaction to the sight of the Muses dictating lugubrious elegy to her favorite pupil is a violent one. She is in no doubt as to the harm they can effect, increasing sickness, accustoming the mind to its illness rather than healing it."[53] In a special category among such female deities is the classical Fortuna.[54] Like Philosophia, this word is also a first-declension feminine noun in Latin, and Fortuna was in fact a Roman goddess. Thomas Bergin has said, commenting on the differences between Dante and Boccaccio:

> In the Middle Ages, deeply religious and darkly superstitious, the study of Fortune's role could not fail to engage the attention

---

[48]*Cons*.II.m.6.15.
[49]*Cons*.III.m.4.4.
[50]*Cons*.II.pr.3.3.
[51]*Cons*.III.m.12.22–23, IV.m.3.4.
[52]*Cons*.I.pr.1.7–11.
[53]Anna Crabbe in Gibson 1981, 249.
[54]Courcelle 1967, 103–111.

of men of intellectual bent or pretension: scholars, churchmen, or poets. Perhaps the crucial question was whether Fortune should be seen as some kind of authorized agent of divinity—God's providence in operation—or as a supreme power, irresponsible and sinister. Dante's answer, given in the sixth canto of the *Inferno*, was clear on this point. For Dante, Fortune was an angel of God, delegated to assure the proper distribution of earthly goods in accordance with the divine will although "oltre la diffension del senno umano," which is to say, beyond the power of men to control or even to comprehend.[55]

Augustine comments polemically on the status of Fortune in Roman religion,[56] and here in his *Consolation of Philosophy* Boethius continues that Augustinian polemic, but in his own special way.[57]

At one point Lady Philosophy refers to Fortuna by the neuter (and neutral) term "divinity [*numen*],"[58] almost as though to avoid feminizing her. But in the descriptions of her, the dialogue does seem to resort to long-standing clichés and canards about feminine wiles and female fickleness, speaking about her "assaults"[59] and reminding Boethius of the times "when she fawned upon thee and allured thee with enticements of feigned happiness."[60] Lady Philosophy's denunciation of the inconstancy and fickleness of Fortune climaxes in a paradox: "I think that Fortune, when she is opposite, is more profitable to men than when she is favorable. For in prosperity, by a show of happiness and seeming to caress [*cum videtur blanda*], she is ever false, but in adversity when she showeth herself inconstant by changing, she is ever true."[61] And therefore, Philosophia advises earlier, "If thou detestest her treach-

---

[55]Bergin 1981, 157, quoting in fact from the seventh canto, *Inf*.VII.81: "oltre la difension d'i senni umani."

[56]Augustine *City of God* IV.18, VII.3.

[57]Murari 1905, 217–297.

[58]*Cons*.II.pr.1.11.

[59]*Cons*.IV.pr.1.2.

[60]*Cons*.II.pr.1.10.

[61]*Cons*.II.pr.8.3.

ery, despise and cast her off, with her pernicious flattery."[62]
Once she is even given the title of *nutrix*, which properly belongs to Philosophy.[63] A more appropriate title than the neuter
word *numen* for Fortuna, consequently, is *domina*, or "sovereign lady": she is the one "whom, of thine own accord, thou
hast chosen for thy sovereign lady";[64] therefore, anyone who
has made such a choice "must be content with the conditions
of thy sovereign lady."[65] A consideration of her "alternations,"
when it is not corrected by a sound teleology, leads to a mis-
understanding of events.[66] For an "unforeseen concourse of
causes" may lead the ignorant to suppose that such events are
the consequence of "chance [*casus*]."[67] But under the rule of
divine Providence "it is placed in your own hands to frame for
yourselves whatever fortune you please."[68] Nevertheless, if she
is correctly understood, in the light of the oxymoron formulated by Philosophia, her rival Fortuna can also become a kind
of teacher in her own right: "In that she deceiveth, in this she
instructeth [*Illa fallit, haec instruit*]."[69]

Yet the diagnosis is not an end in itself: at some point, as
Lady Philosophy says, "Now it is time for the medicine [*medi-
cinae tempus est*]!"[70] She does not, however, administer the
medicine indiscriminately. His "present state of mind," she
notes in Book I, is one in which "this great tumult of emotion
has fallen upon you and you are torn this way and that by
alternating fits of grief, wrath, and anguish"; this, she judges, is
"hardly time for the more powerful remedies."[71] And again, a
bit later: "It is not yet time for stronger medicine."[72] By Book

---

[62] *Cons*.II.pr.1.12.
[63] *Cons*.II.pr.2.4.
[64] *Cons*.II.pr.1.17.
[65] *Cons*.II.pr.1.19.
[66] *Cons*.I.pr.6.19.
[67] *Cons*.V.pr.1.13.
[68] *Cons*.IV.pr.7.22.
[69] *Cons*.II.pr.8.4.
[70] *Cons*.II.pr.2.1.
[71] *Cons*.I.pr.5.11.
[72] *Cons*.I.pr.6.21.

III, however, her medical skill has brought Boethius to the point that he can ask her for such medicine: "You were talking of cures that were rather sharp. The thought of them no longer makes me shudder; in fact I'm eager to hear more, I fervently beg you for them." To this request Lady Philosophy replies: "I knew it! Once you began to hang on my words in silent attention, I was expecting you to adopt this attitude—or rather, to be more exact, I myself created it in you." And then she explains the cure: "The remedies still to come are, in fact, of such a kind that they taste bitter to the tongue, but grow sweet once they are absorbed."[73] And by Book IV she is in a position to apply to him the kinds of remedies that are her specialty. Elsewhere, in connection with the doctrine of the Trinity, Boethius speaks about "the seeds sown in my mind by Saint Augustine's writings [*ex beati Augustini scriptis semina rationum*]."[74] The Augustinianism that Boethius had inherited involved not only the doctrine of the Trinity, but such issues as "the simplicity of providence, the course of fate, sudden chances, God's knowledge and predestination, and free will"; after listing these, Lady Philosophy continues: "It is part of thy cure to know these things also, though the time be short."[75] Then she proceeds to instruct him: "God is the guide and physician of the mind [*rector ac medicator mentium Deus*]."[76]

For because Boethius's work is explicitly intended to be, as its title indicates, a consolation that is provided by philosophy and by reason, not by the Trinitarian theology and Christian doctrine of grace of which Boethius was also a learned and orthodox expositor, Lady Philosophy, even when she is carrying out her ministry as *nutrix*, is at the same time and primarily a *magistra*. It is as both of these that she diagnoses the human predicament with skill and penetration:

The greatest bondage is when, giving themselves to vices, they lose possession of their own reason. For, having cast their eyes

---

[73]*Cons.*III.pr.1.2–3.
[74]Boethius preface to *On the Trinity*.
[75]*Cons.*IV.pr.6.4–5; Courcelle 1967, 203–221.
[76]*Cons.*IV.pr.6.29.

from the light of the sovereign truth to inferior obscurities, forthwith they are blinded with the cloud of ignorance [*inscitia*], molested with hurtful affections, by yielding and consenting to which they increase the bondage which they laid upon themselves, and are, after a certain manner, captives by their own freedom.[77]

In her pupil she confronts a case of profound and self-professed ignorance about all such matters,[78] a "cloudy error of ignorance [*inscitiae nubilus error*]."[79]

> Alas, how thy dull mind is headlong cast
> In depths of woe!

she laments to her pupil.[80] Or, somewhat more harshly, she asks him whether he does not recognize her and, if he does not, whether this is the consequence of *pudor* or of *stupor* on his part, reluctantly concluding that it must be the latter.[81] When he asks her, "Are you joking [*ludisne*]?," she assures him that "we are not joking at all."[82] Because of "the nature of the mind," he has "cast away true opinions" and as a consequence has been "possessed with false" ones.[83] Although he quotes the authority of Socrates to declare that it is not lawful "either to conceal the truth or grant a lie,"[84] he has in fact lost what Socrates regarded as the most important component of knowledge, which is self-knowledge: "You, who in your mind carry the likeness of God, are content to take the ornaments of your excellent nature from the most base and vile things."[85] Nevertheless, "some seed of truth remaineth in our breast," and it is the function of "skillful teaching" to "excite" it into life.[86]

---

[77] *Cons*.V.pr.2.9–10.
[78] *Cons*.III.pr.11.40.
[79] *Cons*.IV.m.5.21.
[80] *Cons*.I.m.2.1–2.
[81] *Cons*.I.pr.2.4.
[82] *Cons*.III.pr.12.30, 12.36.
[83] *Cons*.I.pr.6.21.
[84] *Cons*.I.pr.4.25.
[85] *Cons*.II.pr.5.26.
[86] *Cons*.III.m.11.11–12.

Therefore it is the task of Lady Philosophy as *magistra* to bring her pupil to see the true light.[87] As the one whom "God Himself had inserted in the minds of the wise,"[88] she it is who guides the pupil to recognize what reason persuades the mind to understand about itself.[89] As she says of herself,

> For I have swift and nimble wings
> Which will ascend the lofty skies,
> With which when thy quick mind is clad,
> It will the loathéd earth despise.[90]

When the mind soars this way, it can pray, with Lady Philosophy:

> Dear Father, let my mind Thy hallowed seat ascend,
> Let me behold the spring of grace and find Thy light,
> That I on Thee may fix my soul's well clearéd sight.[91]

The result of such ascending is the restoration to the mind of that self-knowledge which sets human nature apart from the nature of other beings.[92] That will in turn produce in him "the judgment proper to the divine mind."[93] It will as well lead him to be "fully persuaded and convinced by innumerable demonstrations that the souls of men are in no wise mortal," but by nature participate in life eternal.[94]

As Philosophia carries out her teaching duties, she does so "with a soft and sweet voice, observing due dignity and gravity in her countenance and gesture,"[95] with a "sweetness [*mulcedo*]" and a "delightful quality in her singing [*canendi iucunditas*]" that "made me remain astonished, attentive, and

---

[87] *Cons.*IV.pr.1.2.
[88] *Cons.*I.pr.4.8.
[89] *Cons.*III.pr.10.27.
[90] *Cons.*IV.m.1.1–4.
[91] *Cons.*III.m.9.22–24.
[92] *Cons.*II.pr.5.29.
[93] *Cons.*V.pr.5.11.
[94] *Cons.*II.pr.4.28.
[95] *Cons.*IV.pr.1.1.

desirous to hear her longer."[96] She also manifests two womanly qualities that may at first seem paradoxical, but that eventually show their inherent compatibility. One is what Boethius identifies at the beginning as her *imperiosa auctoritas*[97] and near the end as her *dignissima auctoritas*.[98] It is in the exercise of this authority that she assumes the right to instruct, correct, and cajole the greatest living scholar in the Latin West, treating him as a schoolboy and "pupil [*alumnus*]."[99] He in turn addresses her as *magistra*, as in his somewhat plaintive question: "What thinkest thou, O Mistress? Shall I deny this charge, that I may not shame thee?"[100] Later on, when in his confusion he asks, "How can that be?" her response is a schoolmarmish, "Just pay attention [*Attende*]!"[101] Similarly, when in his eagerness he raises new questions that are important but not pertinent to the subject at hand, she warns him against wandering away from "the prescribed course of our study [*a propositi nostri tramite*]" and "getting lost in detours [*deviis fatigatus*]."[102] As an experienced teacher, she finds it necessary to review what has been covered in "our former discourses."[103] She also knows that it is important for the teacher to commend the pupil for his improvement, as he learns to "open his eyes more attentively [*vigilantius*] to discern the truth."[104]

The other womanly quality of Philosophia as *magistra* is her *modesta taciturnitas*. But Boethius describes it as in fact an important element of her pedagogical skill: "After this she remained silent for a while; and, having by that her modesty made me attentive, began in this wise."[105] It would seem that

---

[96]*Cons.*III.pr.1.1–2.
[97]*Cons.*I.pr.1.13.
[98]*Cons.*V.pr.1.2.
[99]*Cons.*III.pr.9.28, 11.40.
[100]*Cons.*I.pr.4.22.
[101]*Cons.*IV.pr.7.2–3.
[102]*Cons.*V.pr.1.1–5.
[103]*Cons.*IV.pr.2.10.
[104]*Cons.*III.pr.12.16.
[105]*Cons.*II.pr.1.1.

at least in part this quality of *modesta taciturnitas* as a pedagogical tactic is related to the humanistic method that Lady
Philosophy employs in her teaching. Her natural habitat, he
says to her, is "the library which thou thyself hadst chosen to
sit in at my house, in which thou hast oftentimes discoursed
with me of the knowledge of divine and human things."[106]
When she first appears to him, she is carrying books.[107] In fact,
however, she does not need his books,[108] since it was she who
had inspired the philosophers to write them. Her discourses
to him here in the *Consolation*, accordingly, are quite book-
ish, not only in the many names of authors and texts that she
cites[109] but in the even greater number to which she refers
without having to cite them by name. Modern-day editors have
had to try to identify these sources, sometimes without suc-
cess.[110] As one scholar has amusingly described the process,
"the Plotinus expert may nail a source for a given phrase only
to have it snatched by a champion of Proclus or Porphyry. On
the other hand many will prefer to take the emphasis right
back to the Platonic original."[111]

Both in her explicit references and in her implicit proce-
dure, the pedagogical process by which Lady Philosophy the
*magistra* carries on such guiding of her pupil Boethius clearly
owes much to the techniques traditionally associated with the
name of Socrates, whom she attended in his life and teaching
and even in his death.[112] "First, therefore," she says to Boethius
in Socratic fashion, "let me touch and try the state of thy mind
by asking thee a few questions," to which he replies: "Ask me
what questions thou wilt, and I will answer thee."[113] From that
point on, as any reader of the Platonic dialogues could have
predicted (and as Boethius, who knew those dialogues very

---

[106] *Cons.* I.pr.4.3.
[107] *Cons.* I.pr.1.6.
[108] *Cons.* I.pr.5.6.
[109] *Cons.* II.m.7.17–20.
[110] The most helpful compilation of this material is Gruber 1978.
[111] Anna Crabbe in Gibson 1981, 239.
[112] *Cons.* I.pr.3.6.
[113] *Cons.* I.pr.6.1–2.

well, also knew very well), the *magistra* will proceed to make the pupil see clearly what has previously been concealed by his "dull mind"[114] and the "stupor" into which he has fallen.[115] In typically Socratic fashion, she interrupts herself in the midst of a lengthy discourse on the eternity of divine foreknowledge to ask Boethius whether human cognition imposes necessity upon events, and then she uses his answer to argue for the harmony of divine foreknowledge and human freedom.[116] Of course, as a good Socratic she claims not to be introducing anything external to his mind at all; to the contrary,

> For being askt how can we answer true
> Unless that grace within our hearts did dwell?
> If Plato's heavenly muse the truth us tell,
> We learning things remember them anew.[117]

To this the pupil replies that he "did very well like of Plato's doctrine, for thou dost bring these things to my remembrance now the second time, because I lost their memory."[118] This is Boethius's version of the Platonic (and Socratic) doctrine of "recollection [ἀνάμνησις]." The most impressive evidence of the author's Platonism is the lengthy summary of Plato's *Gorgias* in Book IV,[119] together with a twenty-eight-line poem in Book III, described by Henry Chadwick as "both the literary climax of the *Consolation* and a major turning point in its argument,"[120] which celebrates the Creator as "goal, beginning, guide, bound, and way [*finis, principium, vector, dux, semita, terminus*]," paraphrasing in meter the central argument in the first part of the *Timaeus* of Plato,[121] that Hellenic

---

[114] *Cons.*I.m.2.1–2.
[115] *Cons.*I.pr.2.4.
[116] *Cons.*V.pr.6.19–21.
[117] *Cons.*III.m.11.13–16.
[118] *Cons.*III.pr.12.1.
[119] *Cons.*IV.pr.2.
[120] Chadwick 1981, 232.
[121] *Cons.*III.m.9.1–28.

counterpart to the Book of Genesis which was to be, in the Latin translation by Chalcidius, what much of early medieval thought had available of the Platonic dialogues. Significantly, it is also the *Timaeus* that Beatrice is obliged to explain and defend in the *Paradiso*.[122]

Despite this decidedly Socratic and Platonic cast of her mind, Philosophia is really quite ecumenical in her judgment about philosophers. And "ecumenical" may be preferable to the more usual (and more disparaging) description of Boethius's philosophy as "eclectic"; for when we meet Philosophia for the first time, her garment is described as having been "cut by the violence of some, who had taken away such pieces as they could get,"[123] which she explains a little later as follows:

> Have we not in ancient times before our Plato's age had oftentimes great conflicts with the rashness of folly? And while he lived, had not his master Socrates the victory of an unjust death in my presence, whose inheritance, when afterward the mob of Epicures, Stoics, and others (every one for his own sect [*pro sua quisque parte*]) endeavored to usurp, and as it were in part of their prey, sought to draw me to them, exclaiming and striving against them; they tore the garment which I had woven with my own hands, and having gotten some little pieces of it, thinking me to be wholly in their possession, departed. Some of whom, because certain signs of my apparel appeared upon them, were rashly supposed to be my familiar friends, and condemned accordingly through the error of the profane multitude.[124]

It will be remembered that before his arrest and imprisonment Boethius had set for himself the task, mind-boggling in the scope of its ambition, of translating all of Plato and all of Aristotle into Latin, and then of creating a harmony of the two systems. To this aborted project the early Middle Ages owed the greater part of what they knew of the genuine writings of

---

[122] *Par*.IV.49–63.

[123] *Cons*.I.pr.1.5.

[124] *Cons*.I.pr.3.6–8.

Aristotle until the coming of Arab learning: the Latin translation of the *Organon*, which caused Aristotle to be known to
early medieval thought chiefly as a logician rather than as a
scientist or ethicist and political theorist or metaphysician.

On the philosophical question from Aristotle's metaphysical
thought that created the greatest difficulty for later medieval
thought, which was the eternity of the world, Boethius confronts the difference between Plato and Aristotle. "They are
deceived," he declares, "who, hearing that Plato thought that
this world had neither beginning of time nor should ever have
an end, think that by this means the created world should be
coeternal with the Creator." [125] It would be fairer to Plato's
thought to reserve the term "everlasting [*aeternus*]" for God
and to call the world only "perpetual [*perpetuus*]." [126] With
Aristotle's doctrine it is more difficult to invoke such a distinction, for "as Aristotle thought of the world, it never began nor
were ever to end, and its life did endure with infinite time";
yet, even here, Boethius seeks to stipulate that for Aristotle the
world "is not such that it ought to be called everlasting." [127] In
keeping with his belief in the essential agreement between
Plato and Aristotle, Boethius has Lady Philosophy here speak
about "Aristoteles meus," referring to the *Physics*. [128] Elsewhere
in his writings, too, Boethius shows how useful the categories
and distinctions of Aristotle are to him, also in the formulation
of his specifically theological thought. Here at the beginning
of the dialogue, Philosophia has similarly gracious things to
say about Canius, Seneca, and Soranus, Roman Stoics who
suffered persecution because they were "instructed in our
school and were altogether disliking to the humors of wicked
men." [129] Near the end of the dialogue, however, she takes a
more polemical stance toward the Stoics as "cloudy old proph-
ets of the Porch." [130]

---

[125] *Cons*.V.pr.6.9. See Augustine *City of God* X.31, XI.4–5.
[126] *Cons*.V.pr.6.14; Courcelle 1967, 221–231.
[127] *Cons*.V.pr.6.6.
[128] *Cons*.V.pr.1.12.
[129] *Cons*.I.pr.3.9–10.
[130] *Cons*.V.m.4.1–2.

Philosophia as *magistra* wants to teach Boethius that "there remaineth also a beholder of all things which is God, who foreseeth all things, and the eternity of His vision, which is always present, concurreth with the future quality of our actions, distributing rewards to the good and punishments to the evil."[131] The doctrine of God she inculcates, therefore, is best expressed in the concept of "the divine understanding [*divina intellegentia*]"[132] and, closely related to it (and following only a few lines later in Book V), "the judgment proper to the divine mind [*divinae iudicium mentis*]."[133] This intellectual metaphor for the divine nature as formulated in Book V appears throughout the *Consolation*, beginning already with Book I. There the universe is described as a "celestial order" framed by the mind of God,[134] and Philosophia celebrates it in verse:

> God every several time
> With proper grace hath crowned
> Nor will those laws confound
> Which He once settled hath.[135]

The mind of God, moreover, is not only the "beginning [*principium*]," but also the "goal [*finis*]" of the universe, toward which "the whole intention of nature tendeth."[136] All of this, and far more, is accessible to human reason if it is set free from ignorance and rightly taught to discern the divine reality, accepting the definition of the divine knowledge as "not an opinion but rather a knowledge grounded upon truth."[137] Yet, at the same time, Lady Philosophy strives to teach the rationalist Boethius about the limitations of reason. There are, she points out, truths of which "scarce any but a contemplator of

---

[131] *Cons.*V.pr.6.45–46.
[132] *Cons.*V.pr.5.8.
[133] *Cons.*V.pr.5.11.
[134] *Cons.*I.pr.4.4.
[135] *Cons.*I.m.6.16–19.
[136] *Cons.*I.pr.6.10–12.
[137] *Cons.*V.pr.6.24.

divinity [*divini speculator*] is capable."[138] The only way to come to terms with the reality of the divine mind is for human reason to recognize that "the divine understanding doth behold future things otherwise than she herself doth."[139] Thus it is characteristic of the human mind to comprehend "by the event of future things [*ex futurarum proventu rerum*]"; by contrast, the divine mind does not comprehend that way, but "by His own simplicity."[140] God's way of knowing is not by composition, as human cognition is, but by "His simple knowledge [*in sua simplici cognitione*]."[141] Although reason, therefore, does have the capacity to know that God is eternal,[142] "the movement of human ratiocination cannot attain to the simplicity of the divine knowledge."[143] To be utterly precise, then, according to the instruction of Lady Philosophy, the language of human reason in speaking about divine reason must be "apophatic," the language of negation.

There is a kind of apostolic succession from Lady Philosophy, Philosophia as Woman, to Lady Beatrice, Theologia as Woman. Although in dealing with the relation of Beatrice to Lady Philosophy "some scholars ... had concluded that, according to Dante, the literal sense of an allegorical poem could contain no historical truth,"[144] there does seem to be some affinity between historical truth and allegory in this portrait of Beatrice. With her "loving voice of comfort [*amoroso suono del mio conforto*],"[145] Beatrice is, in the allegorical vision of Dante, both *nutrix* and *magistra*, in much the same way that Philosophy is for Boethius. She repeatedly tells Dante not to weep, just as Philosophy repeatedly told Boethius.[146]

---

[138]*Cons.*V.pr.6.25.
[139]*Cons.*V.pr.5.8.
[140]*Cons.*V.pr.6.41.
[141]*Cons.*V.pr.6.15.
[142]*Cons.*V.pr.6.1–2.
[143]*Cons.*V.pr.4.2.
[144]Shaw 1938, 26.
[145]*Par.*XVIII.7–8.
[146]*Purg.*XXX.56, XXXI.46; *Cons.*I.pr.4.1, II.pr.4.9.

It is Beatrice who instructs Dante about the stars, and it is Philosophy who instructs Boethius on the same subject.[147] Philosophy's pedagogical use of silence is matched by Beatrice's.[148] Philosophy has "swift and nimble wings," Beatrice gives Dante "wings for your high flight."[149] When Beatrice near the beginning of the *Paradiso* instructs Dante that

> all things, among themselves,
> possess an order; and this order is
> the form that makes the universe like God,

she is telling him something very much like what Philosophy tells Boethius near the beginning of the *Consolation*.[150] Similarly, Philosophy's attempt near the end of the *Consolation* to rule out "determinism [*necessitas*]" in the effort to harmonize divine foreknowledge with human freedom has its counterpart in Beatrice's warning in the *Paradiso* that God's foreknowledge of future contingents "does not imply necessity [*necessità*]."[151] Boethius thanks Lady Philosophy for having banished from his mind "*omnem rerum mortalium cupidinem* [all desire of mortal things]," while Lady Beatrice laments "*cupidigia, che i mortali affonde* [greed, which causes mortals to sink]."[152] And although, in the caution quoted earlier, "it is hard to tell from what source they really came,"[153] there are other similar parallels, above all in the climaxes of the two allegorical visions themselves. Philosophia closes Book II of the *Consolation* with a celebration of that "love which heavenly spheres doth guide [*amor quo caelum regitur*]," and in Book IV she explains to Boethius that under the direction of divine Providence fate in its "course moveth the heaven and

---

[147]*Par*.II.61–148; *Cons*.I.pr.4.4, II.pr.7.3.

[148]*Cons*.II.pr.1.1; *Par*.V.88.

[149]*Cons*.IV.m.1.1; *Par*.XV.54.

[150]*Par*.I.103–105; *Cons*.I.pr.4.4.

[151]*Cons*.V.pr.6.19–24; *Par*.XVII.37–40.

[152]*Cons*.I.pr.4.38; *Par*.XXVII.121.

[153]Patch 1935, 33.

the stars."[154] It does not seem to be straining the parallel to suggest that a conflation of these and other passages in Boethius might lie behind the closing line of the *Divine Comedy*, in which Dante, inspired by Beatrice, celebrates "the Love that moves the sun and the other stars [*l'amor che move il sole e l'altre stelle*]."[155]

---

[154] *Cons*.II.m.8.29–30, IV.pr.6.18.
[155] *Par*.XXXIII.145.

# THREE

# Beatrice as *Donna Mia*

IN the course of reading the *Consolation of Philosophy* upon the death of Beatrice—from his description in the *Convivio*, which was quoted earlier,[1] it was apparently his first reading of the book—Dante seems to have begun a process of conflating Lady Philosophy and Lady Beatrice, who in the *Divine Comedy* and above all in the *Paradiso* takes up into herself many of the attributes and functions of Boethius's Lady Philosophy as *nutrix* and as *magistra*.[2] But there remain many differences between Lady Beatrice and Lady Philosophy. One of the most important is that Beatrice was a genuine person who had lived and (as Dante knew all too well) had died here in this world of time and space, and even and especially in his allegorical treatment of her he never permitted himself to forget it. According to Dante's account in the *Vita Nuova*, "a wonderful vision [*una mirabil visione*] appeared to me, in which I saw things which made me resolve to speak no more of this blessed one, until I could more worthily treat of her." To that end, he continues, "I study to the utmost of my power, as she truly knows." The end result, if all goes well, will be that "if it shall please Him through whom all things live that my life may be prolonged for some years, I hope to say about her what has never been said about any woman [*spero di dire di Lei quello*

---

[1] *Conv.*II.13.
[2] Murari 1905, 255–270.

*che mai non fu detto d'alcuna*]." He saw that hope fulfilled when "that blessed Beatrice [*quella benedetta Beatrice*]" became the Eternal Feminine to whom he dedicated his lifework and about whom he truly did say what has never been said about any woman before or since.[3]

In the case of Beatrice, the counterpoint in Dante's Eternal Feminines between the Eternal and the Feminine, or between the historical and the allegorical, becomes a glorification of the allegorical and transcendent, but one that manages not to lose sight of the inseparable identity between the historical Beatrice Portinari of Dante the man and the allegorical Beatrice of Dante the pilgrim and poet. A striking bit of evidence for Dante's use of this technique appears at one of the high points near the end of the *Paradiso*, when suddenly he sees Beatrice as he has never quite seen her before:

> My seeing nothing else—and love—compelled
> my eyes to turn again to Beatrice.
> If that which has been said of her so far
> were all contained within a single praise,
> it would be much too scant to serve me now.
> The loveliness I saw surpassed not only
> our human measure—and I think that, surely,
> only its Maker can enjoy it fully.[4]

By the time the poet and his reader have reached Canto XXX of the *Paradiso*, "that which has been said of her so far" has become an almost overwhelming accumulation of ideas and images; nevertheless, all of it put together is inadequate to what he sees in her now. Yet that transcendent vision in the upper reaches of paradise, which leaves him "defeated" as a poet and at a loss for words (or, at any rate, since he is who he is, *almost* at a loss for words), becomes the occasion to recall

---

[3] *V.N.*XLI.
[4] *Par.*XXX.14–18.

that first day when, in this life, I saw
her face,[5]

that is, in the spring of 1274 (when both of them were nine),
which he describes in great detail, even to the color of her
dress, in the *Vita Nuova*.[6] When he thinks about Beatrice,
Dante is acutely aware not only of the inadequacy of human
words, but also of the unreliability of human memory "unless
Another is its guide."[7] This is part of the general failure of
memory in relation to transcendent experience, spoken of
also by Saint Paul (whom Dante quotes, though not quite
verbatim):

> I saw things that he
> who from that height descends, forgets or can
> not speak; for nearing its desired end,
> our intellect sinks into an abyss
> so deep that memory fails to follow it.[8]

Nevertheless, as Etienne Gilson has put it, "that Beatrice, a
real woman, was to the poet that was Dante the inexhaustible
source of profound and stimulating emotion . . . is what Dante
himself says in every chapter and almost on every page of the
*Vita Nuova*."[9] The first time he sees her in purgatory, he immediately recollects:

> Within her presence, I had once been used
> to feeling—trembling—wonder, dissolution;
> but that was long ago. Still, though my soul,
> now she was veiled, could not see her directly,
> by way of hidden force that she could move,

[5]*Par.*XXX.28–29.
[6]*V.N.*II.15–18.
[7]*Par.*XVIII.10–12.
[8]*Par.*I.5–9, echoing 2 Cor. 12:2–4.
[9]Gilson 1949, 60.

> I felt the mighty power of old love.
> As soon as that deep force had struck my vision
> (the power that, when I had not yet left
> my boyhood, had already transfixed me),
> I turned around.[10]

Then throughout the Paradiso he repeatedly takes literary pains to speak of her, now in his later years, in the persona of that moonstruck young man he had been then, who would thrill "even on hearing only *Be* and *ice*," the beginning and the end of her name; and yet at the same time he takes even greater pains to emphasize that this name now fills him not only with the romantic "mighty power of old love," but with downright *reverenza*.[11]

Indeed, a close reading of the *Divine Comedy* suggests that to avoid constantly repeating the precious name, and thus running the danger that it might become banal, the poet is on the lookout for synonyms and substitutes, from "admiral" in Canto XXX of the *Purgatorio*[12] to "the sun of my eyes" in the like-numbered canto of the *Paradiso*.[13] By far the most frequent of these substitutes is "my lady," *la donna mia*. She is identified this way already in the *Purgatorio*[14] (and once as *Madonna*,[15] a title that subsequently appears, also only once, in the *Paradiso*).[16] But then *donna* becomes the standard epithet for one canto of the *Paradiso* after another.[17] In several of the cantos, especially, it would seem, in the second half of the *Paradiso*, the title appears twice,[18] and in at least one of

---

[10] *Purg*.XXX.34–43.
[11] *Par*.VII.13–14.
[12] *Purg*.XXX.58.
[13] *Par*.XXX.75: "il sol de li occhi miei."
[14] *Purg*.XXXII.122.
[15] *Purg*.XXXIII.29.
[16] *Par*.II.46.
[17] To cite only some of the more prominent instances: *Par*.V.94, VIII.15, XIV.84, XV.32, XVII.7, XXI.2, XXIII.10, XXVI.68, XXXI.56, XXXII.137.
[18] *Par*.XVII.7, 114, XXV.16, 115, XXVII.76, 89.

them three times.[19] Sometimes there are variations on the title, as, for example, *la bella donna*,[20] or *la dolce donna*,[21] or, more fully, "she, the lady leading me to God."[22] Each repetition has the effect not only of varying the language by which Dante refers to Beatrice, but of reminding the reader, perhaps even reminding the poet, that this allegorical figure and celestial vision not only was, but is, even and especially in what the concluding words of the Nicene Creed call "the life of the age to come [*vita venturi saeculi*]," a woman still, a beautiful woman who continually "grows more beautiful [*far più bella*]"[23] until her beauty surpasses human comprehending or telling,[24] but nonetheless one who in becoming more than a woman must never become less than a woman—one who is, in short, an Eternal Feminine. When Dante describes Beatrice, in purgatory and then in paradise, as having a stance that is "regal and disdainful,"[25] or as "erect [*levata dritta in pè*],"[26] or again as "standing erect, intent,"[27] all of these may well be taken as personal recollections of how she in fact did look when he saw her on earth. But among all the human features of Beatrice the woman are two that, more than any other, carry out this allegorical function:[28] her smile and her eyes, and on several occasions her smile and her eyes in combination as "her smiling eyes [*li occhi suoi ridenti*]."[29]

---

[19]*Par.*XXVIII.40, 61, 86.
[20]*Purg.*XXXIII.121.
[21]*Par.*XXII.100.
[22]*Par.*XVIII.4.
[23]*Par.*VIII.15.
[24]*Par.*XXX.14–18.
[25]*Purg.*XXX.70.
[26]*Purg.*XXXIII.8.
[27]*Par.*XXIII.10–11.
[28]These are, of course, features of other human beings as well as of Beatrice. They appear together, for example, in the pilgrim's words to Justinian (whom Dante does not yet recognize): "I see—plainly—how you have nested in / your own light; see—you draw it from your eyes— / because it glistens even as you smile" (*Par.*V.124–126).
[29]*Par.*X.61–63, III.24, XV.34–36, XVIII.17–21.

In some situations Beatrice's smile functions as a "signal" to the pilgrim,[30] in others as a gentle and amused reproof of him.[31] When she smiles, the planet Mars becomes a "smiling star" and the universe itself seems to be smiling.[32] Her smile is so bright, the poet avers, that it would bring joy to a man "even in fire" (that is, he does seem to be implying, in hell or at least in purgatory, rather than in paradise).[33] As the pilgrim and his Lady Beatrice proceed through paradise together, the smile of Beatrice, like her beauty generally, assumes an increasingly transcendent aspect, as though God's own joy were present in her face.[34] For a while she stops smiling, because, she explains,

> Were I to smile, then you would be
> like Semele when she was turned to ashes,

who, in Ovid's *Metamorphoses*, was incinerated by the unmasked presence of Jupiter. Eventually, however, Dante regains the strength and the composure "to bear the power of [her] smile."[35] Paradoxically, when that smile becomes the most celestial, it is also the most bearable, until, in response to the prayer that Dante addresses to Beatrice in her exalted state, just below Mary and Eve,

> she, however far
> away she seemed, smiled, and she looked at me.

But after having done so, "she turned back to the eternal fountain" of the divine Being.[36]

---

[30] *Par*.XV.71–72.

[31] *Par*.XVI.13–15, with the observations of Cordati Martinelli 1967, 128–129.

[32] *Par*.XIV.79–87, XXVII.4–6.

[33] *Par*.VII.17–18.

[34] *Par*.XXVII.104–105.

[35] *Par*.XXI.5–6 (referring to Ovid *Metamorphoses* III.253–315); *Par*.XXIII.46–47.

[36] *Par*.XXXI.91–93.

The dual role of Beatrice the Eternal Feminine as historical woman and yet simultaneously as theological allegory is, if anything, expressed even more effectively by her eyes than by her smile.[37] "We'll be your guides unto her eyes [*Merrenti a li occhi suoi*]," the handmaids sing to the pilgrim.[38] Already in purgatory she reminisces, in a long discourse about herself and about Dante addressed to "the angels who had been compassionate," on the powerful effect that her eyes have had upon him in his youth, as well as on the changes that have come later:

> My countenance sustained him for a while;
> showing my youthful eyes to him,
> I led him with me toward the way of righteousness.[39]

Now in paradise, her eyes are "holy eyes [*occhi santi*],"[40] as they were called by Faith, Hope, and Charity already in Canto XXXI of the *Purgatorio*.[41] At the same time, he sees in these "holy eyes" of the heavenly Beatrice evidences of her "love [*amor*]" for him.[42] They are the eyes of one who sighs over him as a mother does over a "raving child."[43] Like her smile, her eyes, too, can be a signal that he has her permission to speak.[44] It is by the eyes of Beatrice that Dante is "drawn upward."[45] Together with her smile, "the lovely eyes," which he calls "all beauty's living seals," gain force and become ever more perfect as he and she ascend in paradise.[46] When the pilgrim

---

[37] Ralphs 1959, 20–21.
[38] *Purg.*XXXI.109.
[39] *Purg.*XXX.100–145.
[40] *Par.*III.24.
[41] *Purg.*XXXI.133.
[42] *Par.*XVII.8–9.
[43] *Par.*I.100–102.
[44] *Par.*IX.16–18.
[45] *Par.*XVII.114.
[46] *Par.*XIV.130–139.

> turned to my right side to see if I
> might see if Beatrice had signified
> by word or gesture what I was to do,
> [I] saw such purity within her eyes,
> such joy, that her appearance now surpassed
> its guise at other times, even the last.[47]

And as the heavenly revelations continue to multiply and intensify, it is almost by instinct that the pilgrim's eyes turn again and again to "the fair eyes,"[48] which by this time it has become unnecessary even to identify by Beatrice's name.[49] Significantly, the first time Dante grasps the subtle complexities of the orthodox doctrine of "two natures, but one person" in Christ—the very doctrine on which the emperor Justinian, now in paradise, admits to having been in error while he was on earth, when he permitted himself to be tainted with the Monophysite heresy[50]—he sees it with his own eyes but nonetheless as reflected in the eyes of Beatrice.[51] For she, with her smile and with her eyes, has become "the sun of my eyes."[52]

Like Lady Philosophy in Boethius's *Consolation*, Lady Beatrice acts as Dante's nurse. Therefore, although he opens his prayer with the language of liberation,

> You drew me out from slavery to freedom
> by all those paths, by all those means that were
> within your power,

he soon shifts to medical metaphors reminiscent of the language of the *Consolation* when he prays to her as she sits crowned and enthroned on high:

> Do, in me, preserve
> your generosity, so that my soul,

---

[47] *Par*.XVIII.52–57.
[48] *Par*.XXII.154.
[49] *Par*.XXVIII.11–12.
[50] *Par*.VI.13–21.
[51] *Purg*.XXXI.78, 118–123.
[52] *Par*.XXX.75.

which you have healed, when it is set loose from
my body, be a soul that you will welcome.[53]

A divine and "gentle medicine [*soave medicina*]" is needed to
cure him of his "shortsightedness."[54] "Salvation [*salute*]" in
Dante's Italian still carries the connotation of "health" implied
in the Latin term *salus* from which it is derived, and behind
that in the Greek term σωτηρία. That connotation would
seem not to be absent from Dante's words when he says,
speaking about one of the many times that she cures him of
his faulty vision:

> But, smiling, Beatrice then showed to me
> such loveliness—it must be left among
> the visions that take flight from memory.
> From this my eyes regained the strength to look
> above again; I saw myself translated
> to higher blessedness, alone with my
> lady [*e vidimi translato
> sol con mia donna in più alta salute*].[55]

And so it is fitting that when Dante is struck blind by the overwhelming power of the heavenly Light, he is able to take consolation in being "close to her, and in the world of gladness"
in paradise.[56] But soon the heavenly Voice brings him even
deeper consolation, explaining that

> the woman who conducts you through
> this godly region has, within her gaze,
> that force the hand of Ananias had,

who cured Saul/Paul of the blindness he had incurred when
overwhelmed by the same celestial Light on the road to Da-
mascus in the moment of his miraculous conversion.[57] Her

---

[53] *Par*.XXXI.85–90.
[54] *Par*.XX.139–141.
[55] *Par*.XIV.79–84.
[56] *Par*.XXV.139.
[57] *Par*.XXVI.10–12, referring to Acts 9:1–19.

healing "power [*virtù*]" conquers his "nature" and helps to restore it to the Creator's intention.[58] Lady Beatrice, who acts "for my salvation [*per la mia salute*],"[59] is a heavenly nurse.

But just as Lady Philosophy the *nutrix* functions principally as *magistra* in relation to Boethius in the *Consolation of Philosophy*, so Lady Beatrice the nurse applies her ministrations to Dante chiefly as a teacher throughout the *Paradiso*, addressing herself to the pilgrim's "need to know." Already in purgatory she says to him, shortly after they have joined forces,

> Brother, why not try,
> since now you're at my side, to query me?

to which he responds,

> Lady, you know my need
> to know, and know how it can be appeased.[60]

Therefore, what Dante the poet says about the mental state of Dante the pilgrim near the end of his journey could have been said over and over throughout the entire journey:

> And I, my will rekindled, turning toward
> my lady, was prepared to ask about
> those matters that inclined my mind to doubt.[61]

Because of her special position in relation to God, she possesses authority. Like the Lady Philosophy of Boethius, who carries what he calls *imperiosa auctoritas* and again *dignissima auctoritas*,[62] Lady Beatrice demonstrates her command even over the spirits in paradise.[63] That same authority also

---

[58] *Par*.XXII.102.
[59] *Par*.XXXI.80.
[60] *Purg*.XXXIII.23–24, 29–30.
[61] *Par*.XXXI.55–57.
[62] *Cons*.I.pr.1.13, V.pr.1.2.
[63] *Par*.IX.16–18.

enables her to command Dante: "Shift your thoughts [*Muta pensier*]!"[64] Therefore, in Canto II of the *Paradiso*, she delivers an extended scientific and philosophical lecture, almost a hundred lines long, to correct his mistaken notions about astronomy.[65] Returning to the topic of the stars in a later canto, Dante makes it clear that by now he has learned his lesson about them from Lady Beatrice.[66] Above all, of course, it is not astronomy but theology on which she discourses with such authority, summarizing with a blend of doctrinal precision and poetic eloquence the central argument and the persistent mystery of the doctrine of the Atonement, formulated by Saint Anselm of Canterbury, as the satisfaction that has been rendered to an offended divine justice through the death of Christ.[67]

It is no exaggeration to say that, according to Dante, Beatrice is the recipient of divine inspiration, as a result of which what comes from her mouth is

> the rippling of the holy stream
> issuing from the fountain from which springs
> all truth.[68]

Like the prophet Daniel, therefore, she has received from such divine inspiration the power to interpret dreams.[69] "Give me," the pilgrim asks as though to test her, "proof that you can reflect the thoughts I think."[70] And she does. In Canto VII alone, for example, she reads his mind at least three times.[71] In subsequent cantos she goes on proving to him that "before you think, your thoughts have been displayed" to her.[72] "I tell—not

---

[64] *Par.*XVIII.4–6.
[65] *Par.*II.52–148.
[66] *Par.*XXII.133–141.
[67] *Par.*VII.25–120; Bambeck 1979, 35–38.
[68] *Par.*IV.115–117.
[69] *Par.*IV.13–18.
[70] *Par.*IX.20–21.
[71] *Par.*VII.19–21, 52, 124.
[72] *Par.*XV.63.

ask," she explains imperiously.[73] Sometimes she goes even further, presuming not only to identify his question before he speaks but to "anticipate [his] own reply" and to speak for him.[74] Early on, she provides him with the reason why she, paragon of modesty though she is, takes it upon herself to act with such presumption:

> According to my never-erring judgment [*mio infallibile avviso*]
> ...............................................................................................................................
> I shall quickly free your mind from doubt;
> and listen carefully: the words I speak
> will bring the gift of a great truth in reach.[75]

(Whatever Dante's opinions about papal infallibility may have been, the infallibility of Beatrice is beyond question.) He speaks to the blessed spirits only when she "gives me leave to question you."[76] "By word or gesture" she indicates to him what his duty is.[77] And these are not mere suggestions coming from Beatrice, they are "her commandments."[78] To all of this, therefore, the only proper response from her loving pupil is a "joyful obedience."[79] Eventually, as Beatrice the *magistra* once succeeded Dante's earlier teacher, Virgil, so she is succeeded in turn by one who, while still contemplating, "freely assumes the *officio di dottore*."[80] Saint Bernard of Clairvaux, although he was not to be officially designated a "Doctor of the Church" until the nineteenth century, had begun performing this *officio di dottore* for the entire Western Church already during his lifetime.[81]

Nurse and teacher that she is to him, Dante's Lady Beatrice

---

[73] *Par*.XXIX.10.
[74] *Par*.XXV.51.
[75] *Par*.VII.19, 22–24.
[76] *Par*.XXI.54.
[77] *Par*.XVIII.53–54.
[78] *Purg*.XXXII.107.
[79] *Par*.XXI.22–23.
[80] *Par*.XXXII.1–2.
[81] *Enc.Dant.* 1:601–605.

differs from Boethius's Lady Philosophy in a number of important respects, including the one mentioned earlier, that she is
a human and historical person even while she is functioning
in her capacity as a theological allegory. For the purposes of
the story line of the poem, the most important of the differences between Boethius's Lady Philosophy and Dante's Lady
Beatrice is that as Virgil has led Dante through hell and purgatory, so now Beatrice acts also, and chiefly, as "the lady leading me to God."[82] Lady Philosophy is Boethius's healer and
instructor; Lady Beatrice is Dante's healer and instructor, too.
But while Lady Philosophy is called "our Woman Leader [*nostra dux*],"[83] she does not in fact lead Boethius to any new
places, confined as he is in prison. Beatrice, by contrast, goes
beyond both of the roles of Philosophy as *nutrix* and as
*magistra* to serve as his *guida* through paradise to "the high
goal of your seeking."[84] As he says at the conclusion of the
*Purgatorio,*

> I now returned
> to Beatrice; remade, as new trees are
> renewed when they bring forth new boughs, I was
> pure and prepared to climb unto the stars.[85]

For

> the one who guides me so from good to better
> is Beatrice.[86]

Thus she becomes

> the guide
> who led my feathered wings to such high flight,[87]

---

[82] *Par.*XVIII.4.
[83] *Cons.*I.pr.3.13.
[84] *Par.*XXII.35.
[85] *Purg.*XXXIII.142–145.
[86] *Par.*X.37–38.
[87] *Par.*XXV.49–50.

or, in the words of his ecstatic exclamation: "Oh Beatrice, dolce guida e cara!"[88] Step by step, with her patient explanations and occasionally with her tender reproofs, she heals him and she instructs him, but she also guides him through the circles of paradise, pointing out its splendors to him and introducing him to various of its blessed and "notable [*illustri*]"[89] inhabitants, until

> in beauty ... with voice
> and bearing of a guide whose work is done,[90]

she returns to her place in

> the circle that is third
> from that rank which is highest ... ,
> on the throne her merits have assigned her.[91]

And then the exclamation, "O Beatrice, sweet guide and dear!"[92] is replaced by the plaintive question, "Where is she?!"[93] (which echoes a similarly bewildered question of the pilgrim, "Where is Beatrice?" far earlier, near the end of the preceding cantica).[94]

But the question is replaced in turn by the pilgrim's touching, ardent prayer to Lady Beatrice:

> O lady, you in whom my hope gains strength,
> you who, for my salvation, have allowed
> your footsteps to be left in Hell, in all
> the things that I have seen, I recognize
> the grace and benefit that I, depending
> upon your power and goodness, have received.[95]

---

[88] *Par*.XXIII.34.
[89] *Par*.XXII.20.
[90] *Par*.XXX.34–37.
[91] *Par*.XXXI.67–69.
[92] *Par*.XXIII.34.
[93] *Par*.XXXI.64.
[94] *Purg*.XXXII.85.
[95] *Par*.XXXI.79–84.

It is essential to the entire plot of the *Comedy* and to its meth-
odology that the object of that prayer is, at one and the same
time, the historical Beatrice Portinari, who died on 8 June 1290
and whom Dante had first seen when she was a little girl, and
the *donna mia* of Dante's theological allegory. As Chapters 4
and 5 will seek to show, there is in the *Paradiso* an analogous
identity, and an analogous dialectical tension, between the historical status and the allegorical status both of the Church and
of the Virgin Mary. For his depictions of both of those Eternal
Feminines, however, Dante could find ample documentation
in the Christian tradition, going back to Scripture itself. What
makes the allegory of Beatrice so striking and so audacious is
the literary risk, and even more the theological risk, that he
ran in assigning her such a position in the *Paradiso*—and in
paradise: there was, after all, no Christian doctrine of Beatrice,
as there was—and is—a doctrine of the Church or a doctrine
of Mary. But there certainly was a doctrine of hope in Christian
theology, on which Dante could draw.[96] The famous inscription over the gate of hell, recorded near the very beginning of
the *Divine Comedy*, warns: "Abandon every hope, who enter
here [*Lasciate ogne speranza, voi ch' intrate*]."[97] But she is
permitted to describe Dante in the words,

> There is no child of the Church Militant
> who has more hope than he has [*non ha con più speranza*].[98]

And the pilgrim's prayer to Beatrice recorded near the very
conclusion of the *Divine Comedy*, triumphing over despair,
echoes both that inscription over hell and that description in
paradise by identifying Beatrice as the one "in whom my hope
gains strength [*in cui la mia speranza vige*]."[99]

Dante appears to be acknowledging the risk he is running
here when he confesses that

---

[96] *Enc.Dant.* 5:375–378.
[97] *Inf.*III.9.
[98] *Par.*XXV.52–53.
[99] *Par.*XXXI.79.

in the smile that glowed within her eyes,
I thought that I—and mine—had touched the height
of both my blessedness and paradise
[*de la mia gloria e del mio paradiso*].[100]

For Beatrice is the one "who imparadises [*'mparadisa*] my mind"[101]—a word that would eventually move, at least partly from this source, into English usage as well.[102] On the other hand, it may seem almost as if Beatrice were teasing the lovesick pilgrim when, after

the Eternal Loveliness that shone
on Beatrice directly, from her eyes,
contented me with the reflected light,

she directs his gaze away from herself and toward Cacciaguida, with the admonition:

Turn to him and listen—for
not only in my eyes is Paradise,[103]

and then goes on to remind him in a later canto: "Do you not know you are in Heaven?"[104] Beyond the gentle teasing, however, is the essential characteristic of Beatrice as allegory—indeed, of all three Eternal Feminines as allegories: she is indeed transcendent, and becomes more so as the ascent into paradise progresses, moving from a "brightness" that is almost unbearable already in the early cantos of the *Paradiso*[105] to an incandescent beauty that,

were it not tempered here, would be so brilliant
that, as it flashed, your mortal faculty
would seem a branch a lightning bolt has cracked,[106]

---

[100] *Par.*XV.34–36.
[101] *Par.*XXVIII.3.
[102] *OED* 5–II:74.
[103] *Par.*XVIII.16–21.
[104] *Par.*XXII.7.
[105] *Par.*III.124–130.
[106] *Par.*XXI.10–12; also, for example, already in *Par.*VIII.14–15.

and a "loveliness" exceeding all human measure.[107] But she is also self-transcending, pointing beyond herself to other transcendent realities, and to the ultimate transcendent and all-transcending Reality that is God.

The most explicit signal of this self-transcending quality appears during the pilgrim's ascent into the Fourth Heaven, the Sphere of the Sun.[108] Upon their arrival, Beatrice commands him:

> Give thanks, give thanks
> to Him, the angels' Sun, who, through His grace,
> has lifted you to this embodied sun.

And Dante the pilgrim, as Dante the poet recalls afterward, obeyed her command with alacrity; indeed,

> no mortal heart was ever so disposed
> to worship, or so quick to yield itself
> to God with all its gratefulness, as I
> was when I heard those words.

His "worship" of God and "gratefulness" to God in response to Beatrice's urging were, in their love for God,

> so intent on Him that Beatrice
> was then eclipsed within forgetfulness
> [*Beatrice eclissò ne l'oblio*]—

the same Beatrice about whom the poet's love has been singing so ecstatically. But the feminine Beatrice is an Eternal Feminine, not (or, at any rate not any longer) a mortal burning with jealousy and passion, as Dido had;[109] and therefore

> she was not displeased, but smiled at this,
> so that the splendor of her smiling eyes
> divided my rapt mind between two objects.

---

[107]*Par*.XXX.19–20.
[108]*Par*.X.52–63.
[109]*Par*.IX.97–99.

He clearly means that God is not displeased either, even at being one of these two objects—so long as the other is Beatrice the transcendent but Beatrice the self-transcending.

Hence it is perfectly consistent for Beatrice to join with the heavenly choir:

> a song most sweet
> resounded through that heaven, and my lady
> said with the others: "Holy, holy, holy!" [110]

From its origins in the inaugural vision of the prophet Isaiah, where its text ran, "Holy, holy, holy, is the Lord of hosts: the whole earth is full of his glory," [111] this song had undergone a liturgical evolution into the full text of the Sanctus of the Mass, in which "heaven and earth are full of thy glory," which suited it very well to Dante's purposes in the *Paradiso* and specifically to the self-transcending role of Beatrice in the *Paradiso*. Consequently, when they have reached the Ninth Heaven and the presence of the *Primum Mobile*, it is appropriate that

> Beatrice, a smile upon
> her face, keep silent, even as she gazed
> intently at the Point that overwhelmed me,

a Point beyond Dante and even beyond herself or any other created reality, whether visible or invisible. After this, she breaks her silence by once more pointing beyond herself, as she delivers an exposition of the orthodox Christian doctrine of Creation, including the Creation of the angels, as a *creatio ex nihilo* by a God who, subsisting outside time, called "new loves" into being as objects of "Eternal Love." [112] High on the list of these "new loves"—indeed, "in the seats of the third rank" just below "Eve, so lovely, at Mary's feet" [113]—is Beatrice

---

[110] *Par.*XXVI.67–69.
[111] Isa. 6:3.
[112] *Par.*XXIX.10–48.
[113] *Par.*XXXII.7–9.

herself, whose beauty, by the climax of the *Paradiso*, has become so transcendent

> that, surely,
> only its Maker can enjoy it fully,

and the poet must acknowledge the incapacity of the finite mind to understand or to describe what only the Infinite can know fully.[114] Yet even this ultimate manifestation of Beatrice's transcendence as an Eternal Feminine in the life to come serves to remind him of

> that first day when, in this life, I saw
> her face.[115]

For the historical Beatrice and the *donna mia* of Dante's theological allegory are one, in pointing beyond Beatrice to God.

In the present context it is especially interesting to note the ways in which this one Eternal Feminine, the Lady Beatrice as *donna mia*, points beyond herself to the other two Eternal Feminines: the Bride of Christ, the Church as *bella sposa*; and the Mother of God, the Blessed Virgin Mary as *nostra regina*. It may even be an allusion to the Church as Bride of Christ when Dante describes Beatrice, in the presence of Saint John, as "like a bride, silent and motionless,"[116] but other allusions to the Church are unavoidable. Thus, when Beatrice in the Earthly Paradise prescribes the task to which Dante the poet must set his hand after he has returned to this earth from his pilgrimage, she, "who excluded all things other from my view," charges him to "watch the chariot steadfastly" and to "transcribe" his visions of the Church Triumphant for the benefit of the Church Militant on earth,[117] a Church that has, to such an alarming extent, become not *la bella sposa* but *una*

---

[114] *Par.*XXX.20–24; see already *Par.*I.7–9.
[115] *Par.*XXX.28–29.
[116] *Par.*XXV.111.
[117] *Purg.*XXXII.91–105.

*puttana sciolta*, "wanton harlot," with the pope as her *feroce drudo*, or "savage paramour."[118] Beatrice herself, even in the Heavenly Paradise, still blanches at the shameful sight of this wantonness.[119] But she describes Dante to Saint James as a "child of the Church Militant";[120] and it is she who sings about the Church as a

> fellowship that has been chosen for
> the Blessed Lamb's great supper,

and who, as the "holy sister" of Saint Peter, recommends Dante to him.[121] The poet's last vision of her (and our last vision of her) is in the setting of the Church Triumphant: "Beatrice con quanti beati."[122]

A dominant component of those closing visions in the *Paradiso* is the Heavenly Rose.[123] Dante describes how

> into the yellow of the eternal Rose
> that slopes and stretches and diffuses fragrance
> of praise unto the Sun of endless spring
> now Beatrice drew me.[124]

From the lines that follow soon after that description it is clear that, at least here, Dante means by

> that white Rose, the holy
> legion . . . the host that Christ,
> with His own blood, had taken as His bride,[125]

namely, the Church Triumphant. But elsewhere the metaphor of the Rose no less clearly means Mary,

---

[118]*Purg.*XXXII.149, 155.
[119]*Par.*XXVII.31–36.
[120]*Par.*XXV.52.
[121]*Par.*XXIV.1–2, 29.
[122]*Par.*XXXIII.38.
[123]Di Scipio 1984 is an analysis of the complexity of this image.
[124]*Par.*XXX.124–127.
[125]*Par.*XXXI.1–3.

> the Rose in which the Word of God became
> flesh,

as Beatrice calls her when she chides Dante for being "so en-
raptured by my face" that he fails to pay sufficient attention to
the Garden and the Rose.[126] The allegorical or typological
identification between Mary and the Church, for which there
is a great body of precedent in patristic and medieval tradition,
is relevant here as an index to the self-transcending vocation
of Beatrice, who points beyond herself to both of them. Near
the very beginning of the *Comedy*, Mary calls on Lucia, who in
turn calls on Beatrice, to help Dante.[127] Near the very end of
the *Comedy*, in the same way but in a tone that is even more
sublime and exalted, Canto XXXI of the *Paradiso* brings Beatrice and the Blessed Virgin together, but it juxtaposes them
in such a manner that the self-transcendence of Beatrice is fulfilled in the heavenly figure of Mary. Therefore, Beatrice is
described by Saint Bernard of Clairvaux as part of the com-
munion of saints in the Church Triumphant, where she and
they are engaged in an eternal prayer to Mary as *regina*.[128]

---

[126] *Par.*XXIII.70–75.
[127] *Inf.*II.94–108.
[128] *Par.*XXXIII.34–39.

# FOUR

# The Church as *Bella Sposa*

It was during the lifetime of Dante Alighieri that the doctrine of the Church, after a previous history that can best be described as episodic, moved to the center of theological attention in the Latin West, a position it was to occupy for approximately three centuries. There is no tractate "On the Church" in the *Summa Theologica* of Saint Thomas Aquinas, nor is there a set of questions on the definition of the Church in the most widely used theological textbook of the Middle Ages (on which there exist more than two thousand commentaries), the four books of the *Sentences* of Peter Lombard. Just as the fourteenth century was beginning, there appeared what Henri Xavier Arquillière has called "the oldest treatise on the Church," written by James of Viterbo;[1] and from then on the nature of the Church was to dominate the theological agenda, through the period of the Protestant Reformation and well beyond it, only to recede from attention again until the renewal of ecclesiology in the nineteenth and twentieth centuries. Dante himself made a significant contribution to the development of the doctrine of the Church in the later Middle Ages with his treatise *De Monarchia*. Yet it must be conceded that his most complete statements about the doctrine of the Church came in the *Divine Comedy*.[2]

Now when a child of the Western Christian tradition such as

---

[1] Arquillière 1926.
[2] See Guzzo 1959, 26–42: "Dante e la Chiesa."

Dante took up the doctrine of the Church, he could draw upon the tradition for a rich variety of terms and metaphors in which the doctrine had been expressed by Scripture, by the creeds and councils, and by the doctors of the Church.[3] And that is precisely what Dante does, above all in the *Paradiso*, where the Church in heaven and on earth is identified by a plenitude of titles and metaphors, describing it, inter alia, as "the ancient and the new council" in Old Testament and New,[4] or as "the bark of Peter."[5] Some of these metaphors are liturgical: "our basilica";[6] the "fellowship" at "the Blessed Lamb's great supper";[7] and the "sweet lyre" on which God plays "consecrated chords."[8] Some are horticultural: "this fair flower [*questo fior venusto*]";[9] "the good plant—once a vine and now a thorn";[10] the "vineyard" that now "withers when neglected by its keeper";[11] "the beautiful garden,"[12] or "the Catholic garden,"[13] or, more explicitly, the "garden" of Christ.[14] And still others are social or political: "the Christian people [*popol cristiano*]";[15] the "realm" or kingdom of God;[16] "this court [*questa corte*]," where God is the "Emperor" and the saints are the "nobles";[17] "this most just and merciful empire";[18] "the holy forum";[19] and "Christ's army."[20]

---

[3] *Enc.Dant.*1:960–968.

[4] *Par.*XXIII.138.

[5] *Par.*XI.119–120.

[6] *Par.*XXV.30.

[7] *Par.*XXIV.1–3; see also XIII.31.

[8] *Par.*XV.4–6.

[9] *Par.*XXXII.126.

[10] *Par.*XXIV.110–111.

[11] *Par.*XII.86–87.

[12] *Par.*XXIII.71, XXXII.39.

[13] *Par.*XII.104.

[14] *Par.*XII.72.

[15] *Par.*XXVII.48.

[16] *Par.*XXIV.43.

[17] *Par.*XXV.40–43.

[18] *Par.*XXXII.117.

[19] *Par.*XXX.142.

[20] *Par.*XII.37.

One of the most important of all such terms comprehending the Church in heaven and on earth is the traditional distinction[21] between the *ecclesia militans*, the Church Militant here below (which Dante calls "la Chiesa militante"),[22] and the *ecclesia triumphans*, the Church Triumphant above (which Dante describes Beatrice as calling "le schiere del triunfo di Cristo").[23] The distinction between Church Militant and Church Triumphant has many affinities with Augustine's distinction between the City of Earth and the City of God; but because in the Augustinian distinction the Church is, in some sense, the City of God already as Church Militant, and not only as Church Triumphant, the distinctions are not identical. And although the distinction is at work in the *Inferno* and in the *Purgatorio*, it is only in the *Paradiso*, with its description of Dante's vision of the Church Triumphant, that the opposition between the Church in heaven and the Church on earth truly comes into its own, because it is only here that empirical Christendom, the Church Militant on earth, can be judged on the basis of the sign and paradigm to which it pledges its allegiance every day in the Credo of the Mass: "Et in unam sanctam catholicam et apostolicam Ecclesiam"—words that were, by what Dante clearly regarded as a grim irony, echoed in the title and opening of the bull *Unam Sanctam* issued by Pope Boniface VIII on 18 November 1302.[24]

"The Rose is a cathedral; it is the 'Ecclesia Triumphans,' " a recent study has declared.[25] Dante's language about the Church Triumphant begins to become explicit in Canto XXIII of the *Paradiso*, when Beatrice says to the pilgrim:

> There you see the troops
> of the triumphant Christ![26]

---

[21] *S.T.* Ia IIae.102.4 *ad* 3.

[22] *Par.*XXV.52.

[23] *Par.*XXIII.19–20.

[24] Rivière 1926, 79–91, 150–155.

[25] Di Scipio 1984, 159.

[26] *Par.*XXIII.19–20.

The poet adds that, as she said these words, Beatrice's

> face was all aflame,
> and there was so much gladness in her eyes
> I am compelled to leave it undescribed.[27]

The Church Militant on earth, like the individual believer, is characterized by "suspense and longing," and in its desire must be "satisfied with hope [*sperando s' appaga*]."[28] The reference to a hope that still looks to the future and that nevertheless is already "satisfied" unavoidably recalls the final line of the inscription over the entrance to hell,[29] as well as the many variations on the theme of "hope [*speranza*]" throughout the poem.[30] Paradise is the object of the hope of Christian pilgrims now in the Church Militant, and it will be the fulfillment of that hope forever in the Church Triumphant. It would, however, be a mistake in reading the *Paradiso* to concentrate on "hope" and "fulfillment" in such a way as to overlook the related, but not identical, dualism of "longing" and "satiety," which is also an important element in Dante's ecclesiology. Within the *Paradiso* the dualism of satiety and longing apears in dramatic form in the words of Beatrice that open Canto XXIV:

> O fellowship that has been chosen for
> the Blessed Lamb's great supper, where He feeds
> you so as always to fulfill your need,
> since by the grace of God, this man receives
> foretaste of something fallen from your table
> before death has assigned his time its limit,
> direct your mind to his immense desire,
> quench him somewhat: you who forever drink
> from that Source which his thought and longing seek.[31]

---

[27] *Par*.XXIII.22–24.
[28] *Par*.XXIII.13–15.
[29] *Inf*.III.9.
[30] Lovera 1975, 3:2293.
[31] *Par*.XXIV.1–9.

It is certainly correct, with many commentators, to recall, in this description of the heavenly banquet, the words of the poet to his readers early in the *Paradiso*, after warning them not to view the journey frivolously as a kind of lark, but to turn back from it now if they are not ready for its burden, for "the waves I take were never sailed before." Thereupon he turns from the frivolous crowd to the serious elite:

> You other few who turned your minds in time
> unto the bread of angels, which provides
> men here with life—but hungering for more.[32]

These few are the ones whom Dante encourages to continue the journey with him; for their "hungering for more" while still in the Church Militant has prepared them for "the Blessed Lamb's great supper" in the Church Triumphant and for "the bread of angels," which is the heavenly wisdom. Thus, the distinction between Church Militant and Church Triumphant appears in several aspects of Dante's interpretation of the Church and of its life.

Yet even that distinction, upon which the poet does draw extensively in the *Paradiso*, is not adequate to the task that Dante sets for himself in describing the Church as both the Church in heaven and the Church on earth. When, therefore, at the opening of Canto XXXI, he speaks of seeing the Church as "the holy legion [*la milizia santa*]," the army that was the Church Militant on earth and that now is the Church Triumphant in heaven, he immediately shifts from this metaphor to another: "the host that Christ, with His own blood, had taken as His bride [*che nel suo sangue Cristo fece sposa*]."[33] Sometimes, echoing the Song of Songs, Dante speaks of the Church as

> the Bride of God, [who] on waking, sings
> matins to her Bridegroom, encouraging
> His love.[34]

---

[32] *Par.* II.1–15.
[33] *Par.* XXXI.2–3.
[34] *Par.* X.140–141.

But in the title "Bride of Christ" Dante strikes upon the metaphor that is in many ways his most appropriate one of all for the Church in heaven and on earth, because no other term, not even "the good plant—once a vine and now a thorn,"[35] can describe with such desperate poignancy both the glory and the shame manifested by a Church that was selected to be the Bride of Christ and that has now become a harlot. "Bride of Christ" is uniquely equipped to articulate what we have been calling here the counterpoint between the Eternal and the Feminine, between the historical and the allegorical.[36] And since it is "the Church which is the ultimate allegory,"[37] the Church as

> the Bride of Him who, with loud cries,
> had wed her with His blessed blood[38]

can take her place among the allegorical Eternal Feminines of the *Paradiso*, along with Beatrice and Mary. Dante describes Beatrice as looking "just like a bride,"[39] and he refers to Mary as

> the only bride
> the Holy Ghost has known.[40]

Although it is striking, and admittedly somewhat surprising, to note how seldom the poet uses the term "bride" in any sense,[41] these passages show that he does apply the metaphor to all three Eternal Feminines.

It is, on the other hand, not surprising that Dante echoes the

---

[35]*Par*.XXIV.110–111.

[36]Newman 1987, 196–249, is rich with insights into the metaphor "Bride of Christ" as expounded by Saint Hildegard.

[37]Rand 1928, 89.

[38]*Par*.XI.32–33.

[39]*Par*.XXV.111.

[40]*Purg*.XX.97–98.

[41]Lovera 1975, 3:2304, lists only fourteen references to "sposa" in the entire *Divine Comedy*, more than half of them, significantly, occurring in the *Paradiso*.

traditional medieval usage of characterizing a nun as a bride of Christ,[42] but it is significant that the only other extended use he makes of the bridal metaphor in the *Paradiso* is in Cantos XI and XII, which deal with Saint Dominic and Saint Francis.[43] Dominic, it is said, completed his espousal with "the Faith [*la Fede*]" already at his baptism, with "mutual salvation as their dowry."[44] But it seems plausible that Dante is invoking the bridal metaphor in speaking about Dominic in Canto XII chiefly for the sake of achieving balance with the lengthy narrative in the previous canto, where he has asked his readers to

> take Francis and take Poverty
> to be the lovers meant in my recounting.[45]

Reflecting a tradition that apparently goes back to Francis himself and that is immortalized in the fresco attributed to Giotto, *The Marriage of Saint Francis and Poverty*, in the lower basilica of San Francesco at Assisi,[46] Dante develops this metaphor in considerable detail, which includes the image of Poverty as Bride of Christ. Francis, he says, "ran to war" as a young man in the service of Lady Poverty. For eleven centuries, after having lost "her first husband," she had been without a suitor, "scorned" and "obscure," until Francis, who "loved her more day by day," took her as his bride.[47] Her "first husband" was, of course, Christ himself, who had been the first to embrace Lady Poverty, as Francis was now only the second one to do so. But from Dante's juxtaposition, which surely cannot be accidental, of the metaphor of Poverty as Bride of Christ with that of the Church as Bride of Christ (which appears fewer than thirty lines earlier in the same canto)[48] it seems safe to

---

[42] *Par.* III.97–102.
[43] Needler 1969, 26–30.
[44] *Par.* XII.61–63.
[45] *Par.* XI.74–75.
[46] Weigelt 1925, 159.
[47] *Par.* XI.58–66.
[48] *Par.* XI.28–36.

conclude that also in this disquisition on poverty the poet is making a point which is primarily ecclesiological, and that he is doing so in the context of the poverty controversies of the fourteenth century.[49]

The ecclesiological point, moreover, is being expressed by drawing a striking contrast between the Church as bride and the Church as harlot. This contrast seems to be the one ecclesiological metaphor that runs through all three cantiche of Dante's *Divine Comedy*, successfully bringing together the Church in heaven and the Church on earth—but bringing them together by radically distinguishing between them. Already in Canto XIX of the *Inferno* Dante opens with a denunciation of the

> rapacious ones, who take the things of God,
> that ought to be the brides of Righteousness,
> and make them fornicate for gold and silver![50]

Later in that canto he has Nicholas III, Pope from 1277 to 1280, cry out when he recognizes Boniface VIII and identifies him by name (the first and only time that this name, which Dante clearly regards as an abomination, is mentioned in the entire *Divine Comedy*):[51]

> Are you already standing,
> already standing there, o Boniface?
> The book has lied to me by several years,[52]

because Boniface was not supposed to arrive until two decades after Nicholas.[53] Then Pope Nicholas assails his successor:

---

[49]Lambert 1961.

[50]*Inf.*XIX.2–4.

[51]*Enc.Dant.* 1:675–679.

[52]*Inf.*XIX.52–54.

[53]Assuming that *lo scritto* referred to by Nicholas pertains to the book of life and book of the future, known to the dead, rather than to some medieval apocalyptic treatise.

> Are you so quickly sated with the riches
> for which you did not fear to take by guile
> the Lovely Lady [*la bella donna*], then to violate her?[54]

—a reference to the illegal means that Boniface was alleged to have employed in securing the papacy. After that, to set the Church as bride into the sharpest possible opposition with what Boniface has done to her, Dante the pilgrim begins to speak in the language of the Apocalypse of Saint John the Divine:

> You, shepherds, the Evangelist [John] had noticed
> when he saw her who sits upon the waters
> and realized she fornicates with kings,
> she who was born with seven heads and had
> the power and support of the ten horns,
> as long as virtue was her husband's pleasure.[55]

The "shepherds" and pastors of the Church on earth are to remind themselves of the vision of the harlot in the Apocalypse.

Again in Canto XXXII of the *Purgatorio*, which is similarly filled with images from the Apocalypse, Dante the pilgrim— and, with him, the reader of Dante the poet—is being prepared, on the basis of the contemplation of the Earthly Paradise, for the contemplation of the Church as the Bride of Christ in the Heavenly Paradise. Into this canto's complex zoological imagery of the griffin, the eagle, the fox, and the dragon there is now interposed another and far more disturbing image, the obscene vision of a Church that has gone wrong and of the one who is responsible for her downfall:

> Just like a fortress set on a steep slope,
> securely seated there, ungirt, a whore,
> whose eyes were quick to rove, appeared to me;
> and I saw at her side, erect, a giant,

---

[54]*Inf.*XIX.55–57.
[55]*Inf.*XIX.106–110.

> who seemed to serve as her custodian;
> and they—again, again—embraced each other.
> But when she turned her wandering, wanton eyes
> to me, then that ferocious amador
> beat her from head to foot.[56]

The "puttana sciolta," familiar from the Book of Revelation, is the Church in her shame and corruption, whose "eyes," by contrast with the holy eyes of Beatrice, are "wandering" and "wanton"; and the "gigante" whose function it ought to be "to serve as her custodian" but who instead "beats her from head to foot" may be the pope, Boniface VIII, whom she permits to fondle her "again, again" (although the "custodian" may refer to Philip IV, who "dragged" the papacy to Avignon). No other image of the Church, among the many that Dante employs on the basis of Scripture and tradition, can simultaneously evoke both her grandeur and her misery so dramatically. In the closing vision of paradise the pilgrim sees, among others, Saint John the Divine, the author of the Book of Revelation,

> who saw, before he died, all of
> the troubled era of the lovely Bride.[57]

The Book of Revelation comes to its highest point with the vision of the Church, in which "I John saw the holy city, new Jerusalem, coming down from God out of heaven, prepared as a bride adorned for her husband."[58] Its lowest point, moreover, is reached in yet another vision of a woman, "the great whore that sitteth upon many waters," who is "drunken with the blood of the saints, and with the blood of the martyrs of Jesus," and on whose forehead the name stands written, "Mystery, Babylon the great, the mother of harlots and abominations of the earth."[59] It is the dazzling achievement of the

---

[56] *Purg.*XXXII.148–156.
[57] *Par.*XXXII.127–128.
[58] Rev. 21:2.
[59] Rev. 17:1–6.

literary genius—and theological genius—of Dante in his theological allegory of the Church in heaven and on earth, as bride and as harlot, to have conflated these two images of the Apocalypse, which evidently are altogether distinct in the Book of Revelation itself.

Having prepared his reader for this shocking chiaroscuro in Canto XIX of the *Inferno* and then in Canto XXXII of the *Purgatorio*, Dante can build up the image in successive cantos of the *Paradiso*, until the next to the last.[60] For example, in introducing the description of the "two princes [*due principi*]" who were divinely appointed to guide the Church, Saint Dominic and Saint Francis, Dante identifies it as the ministry of Francis through his marriage to Lady Poverty,[61] as well as the mission of Dominic through his marriage to the Faith,[62] to enable the Bride of Christ to "meet her Love with more fidelity and more assurance in herself [*in sé sicura e anche a lui più fida*]," that is, with the fidelity of faith and the security of poverty.[63] Clearly the marital fidelity of this bride to this bridegroom, like his fidelity to her, is a pearl of great price; and by the same count her infidelity to him is the betrayal of a relationship that is not only human but divine, not only of this world but also of the world to come. That is what makes her one of "those who, in the world, go most astray";[64] as the scholastic epigram has it, "*corruptio optimi pessima* [there is nothing worse than the corruption of the best]." After employing in at least two passages the Old Testament metaphor of the "noble vine" that has now been "turned into the degenerate plant of a strange vine,"[65] Dante the poet recurs to the metaphor of the bride and the harlot, heightening its dramatic effectiveness in the poem by portraying it in a mirror image that Dante the pilgrim sees reflected in the face of Beatrice. At Saint Peter's grim de-

---

[60] *Par*.XXXII.124–129.
[61] *Par*.XI.61–75.
[62] *Par*.XII.61–63.
[63] *Par*.XI.28–36.
[64] *Par*.XVI.58.
[65] *Par*.XII.86–87, XXIV.110–111; see Jer. 2:21.

nunciation of the Church on earth in the name of the Church in heaven, climaxing in the assertion that the demonic powers are lodged in the Church on earth because

> the perverse one who fell from Heaven, here
> above, can find contentment there below,[66]

the heavens blush as they did for three hours at noon on Good Friday when Christ expired, and Beatrice is visibly shaken:

> And like a woman who, although secure
> in her own honesty, will pale on even
> hearing about another woman's failing,
> just so did Beatrice change in appearance;
> and I believe that such eclipse was in
> the sky when He, the Highest Power, suffered.[67]

Then Peter, as if to confirm the theological validity of such audacious language, once again identifies the Church as "the Bride of Christ [*la sposa di Cristo*]," purchased by the blood of Christ but nurtured also by the blood of the martyrs, including his own as well as that of Popes Linus and Cletus.[68] The allegorical contrast between the bride and the harlot, in turn, provides the framework for Dante's depiction of the other contrasts between the Church on earth and the Church in heaven.

This exchange with Saint Peter, when read in the light of the dramatis personae to whom the reader has been introduced throughout the *Inferno* and the *Purgatorio*, suggests that the most remarkable of the contrasts between the Church on earth and the Church in heaven is probably the difference between the hierarchies of the two.[69] The analogy between the two hierarchies had been the preoccupation of the unknown author

---

[66] *Par.*XXVII.26–27.
[67] *Par.*XXVII.31–36.
[68] *Par.*XXVII.40–41.
[69] *Enc.Dant.* 1:268–272.

of the late fifth or early sixth century who wrote under the
name of Dionysius the Areopagite, the convert of the apostle
Paul in Athens mentioned in the seventeenth chapter of the
Book of Acts; Pseudo-Dionysius composed a book called *The
Ecclesiastical Hierarchy* and another called *The Celestial Hierarchy*. Dante's catalog of theologians in the Fourth Heaven
enumerated by Thomas Aquinas celebrates Dionysius the Areopagite as

> that candle
> which, in the flesh, below, beheld most deeply
> the angels' nature and their ministry.[70]

And, in a later canto of the *Paradiso*, Thomas Aquinas names
him as

> Dionysius, [who], with much longing set
> himself to contemplate these [angelic] orders: he
> named and distinguished them just as I do,

in opposition to Pope Gregory the Great, whose ordering of
the angelic hierarchy Dante himself had earlier followed in the
*Convivio*[71] but has now revised to conform to the angelology
of Dionysius and of Saint Thomas. When Gregory came to
paradise and discovered that Dionysius had been right after
all, Dante suggests, he "smiled at his mistake"—as, one can
imagine, does Dante himself, now that Beatrice, in agreement
with Dionysius the Areopagite, has corrected the mistaken
theories of the *Convivio*.[72]

Canto XXVIII of the *Paradiso* is a review of the nine circles
of the celestial hierarchy in three triads, as described by
Pseudo-Dionysius. The nine circles are, in ascending order (although here in Canto XXVIII Dante lists them in descending

---

[70]*Par*.X.115–117.
[71]*Conv*.II.6.
[72]*Par*.XXVIII.130–135.

order): the angels playing their "games [*Angelici ludi*],"[73] the archangels, the "principalities [*Podestadi*]," the powers, the virtues, the dominions, the thrones, the cherubim, and the seraphim. The number of the celestial hierarchy, Dante tells us, "ran to more thousands than the doubling of the chessboard [*più che 'l doppiar delli scacchi s'inmilla*],"[74] a reference to the ancient legend that the inventor of the game of chess requested from the king of Persia, as his reward for this boon to humanity, one grain of wheat for the first square on the board, twice that for the second, twice that in turn for the third, and so on for all sixty-four squares: which comes, it has been computed, to about eighteen and one-half billion billion grains—and, by one possible interpretation of the words "s'inmilla," Dante may even be read as saying that the number of the angels would be a thousand times that. As a chapter in medieval intellectual history, this disquisition on the angels provides important evidence about Dante's relation to his sources—above all of course to Pseudo-Dionysius, but also to Thomas Aquinas, whose exposition "Of the Angelic Degrees of Hierarchies and Orders" in the *Summa Theologica* had anticipated Dante's (and Beatrice's) in preferring Dionysius the Areopagite to Gregory the Great. For, Thomas explains, "Dionysius explains the names of the orders according as they befit the spiritual perfections they signify; Gregory, on the other hand, in expounding these names, seems to regard more the exterior ministrations."[75]

In the present context, however, Dante's description of the celestial hierarchy of the Church in heaven, the Bride of Christ, stands in the sharpest possible antithesis with the treatment he has been according to the ecclesiastical hierarchy of the Church on earth. For he introduces it, in the opening lines of Canto XXVIII, with words about

---

[73] *Par.*XXVIII.126.
[74] *Par.*XXVIII.92–93.
[75] *S.T.*I.108.5.

> the truth that is unlike
> the present life of miserable mortals,[76]

namely, the truth that has just been revealed to him in the preceding Canto XXVII. There Beatrice has denounced the mortal
sin of "*cupidigia* [covetousness, or greed]," which drowns
mortals in its ocean depths until none can see above its
waves.[77] No one is immune to the seductive allure of covetous-
ness, and at the beginning of Canto XXVII Dante puts into
the mouth of none other than Saint Peter, the Prince of the
Apostles and the first pope, now translated into the Church
Triumphant in heaven, a mournful lament over the state of the
Church Militant on earth. Peter knows at first hand what it
means to deny the Lord Jesus Christ while on earth, but he has
come to the Church Triumphant through the trial of martyrdom by crucifixion (upside down, the legend had it, so as not
to make himself equal to Christ). Now, looking at the Church
Militant, he complains, in words that have been quoted earlier,
about what has happened to the "Bride of Christ."[78] The jere-
miad continues, recalling the words in which the *Inferno* at-
tacks Pope Boniface VIII (though without naming him):

> The prince of the new Pharisees
> . . . . . . . . . . . . . . . . . . . . . . . . . . . . . . . . . . . . . . .
> took no care for the highest office or
> the holy orders that were his.[79]

Here in paradise—looking down "from here on high," from
the perspective of the Church in heaven upon the Church on
earth with its "rapacious wolves clothed in the cloaks of shepherds"—Saint Peter,

---

[76]*Par*.XXVIII.1–2.
[77]*Par*.XXVII.121–123.
[78]*Par*.XXVII.40–42.
[79]*Inf*.XXVII.85, 91–92.

> with a voice so altered
> from what it was before—even his likeness
> did not display a greater change than that,

laments the betrayal in language that is even more bitter:

> We did not want one portion of Christ's people
> to sit at the right side of our successors,
> while, on the left, the other portion sat,
> nor did we want the keys that were consigned
> to me, to serve as an escutcheon on
> a banner that waged war against the baptized;
> nor did we want my form upon a seal
> for trafficking in lying privileges—
> for which I often blush and flash with anger.

The anger causes him to cry out with holy impatience, even though he is here in eternal glory:

> You, the vengeance
> of God, oh, why do you still lie concealed?

Peter closes his oration with a charge to Dante the pilgrim that was to be carried out by Dante the poet:

> And you, my son, who through your mortal weight
> will yet return below, speak plainly there,
> and do not hide that which I do not hide.[80]

Dante carries out that charge by using the "truth" of the Church in heaven, the Bride of Christ,

> the truth that is unlike
> the present life of miserable mortals,[81]

---

[80] *Par.*XXVII.37–66.
[81] *Par.*XXVIII.1–2.

to call the harlot Church on earth to account and to summon it to reform. He speaks from the conviction that despite all appearances the reform of the Church is still possible, for the papacy has "gone astray" and become corrupt "not in itself [where it remains the bark of Peter],[82] but in its occupant."[83] Unlike some critics of his own and of later centuries, Dante is one of those who "view the nature and function of the priesthood and papacy from the standpoint of the Christian faith alone";[84] therefore, he does not write off the institutional Church altogether but laments and denounces it in the name of what Christ intended the Church to be in making it his bride.

One pillar of the authority of the hierarchical Church Militant on earth and of its domination over the political rulers of the temporal empire was the ecclesiastical legislation assembled in the various collections of medieval canon law. It should be noted that the vast majority of the popes of the Middle Ages had come to their high office after studying canon law rather than scholastic theology—not to mention liturgical theology or biblical exegesis. So dominant was the role that canon law played in medieval thought that most of what was said about the nature of the Church during the Latin Middle Ages was not said by the theologians but by the canon lawyers. The term "body of Christ [*corpus Christi*]" in the New Testament and the liturgical image of the "mystical body [*corpus mysticum*]" in the church fathers provided a justification for treating the Church as a "corporation" under law. The profound and scholarly study of the question by Ernst Kantorowicz has summarized the development this way:

The mysterious materiality which the term *corpus mysticum*— whatever its connotations may have been—still harbored, has

---

[82]*Par*.XI.119–120.
[83]*Par*.XII.89–90.
[84]Gewirth 1951, 43.

been abandoned: "The *corpus Christi* has been changed into a corporation of Christ." It has been exchanged for a juristic abstraction, the "mystical person," the *persona repraesentata* or *ficta*, which the jurists had introduced into legal thought and which will be found at the bottom of so much of the political theorizing during the later Middle Ages. Undeniably the former liturgical concept of *corpus mysticum* faded away only to be transformed into a relatively colorless sociological, organological, or juristic notion.[85]

As he adds, "this 'degeneration' made itself felt very strongly in the circle of theologians around Pope Boniface VIII."

Yet Dante, who is the implacable enemy of Boniface VIII, and who in the *Paradiso* praises the devotion of Saint Francis to the Church as "vineyard," by comparison with those who work "for the world" by their cultivation of canon law,[86] also puts the "father of canon law" into the company of the theologians in the Fourth Circle of Heaven:

> Gratian,
> who served one and the other court of law [canon law and civil law]
> so well that his work pleases Paradise,

and whom Dante therefore portrays as smiling.[87] From the third book of the *De Monarchia* it is clear that Dante regarded it as a blight that the canon lawyers, "ignorant of any kind of theology and philosophy," should exercise such a tyranny over the life and mind of the Church on earth.[88] He recognized that it was possible to trace to them much of the political ambition in the Church that was the source both of weakness in the empire and of corruption in the papacy.[89] Yet here, in describing

---

[85] Kantorowicz 1957, 202.
[86] *Par*.XII.82–87.
[87] *Par*.X.103–105.
[88] *Mon*.III.3.
[89] Maccarone 1951.

the Church in heaven, he exalts Gratian into the company
of the Venerable Bede and Isidore of Seville, and even that of
Thomas Aquinas and Albertus Magnus. To the resolution of
this apparent contradiction the distinction between the Church
on earth and the Church in heaven makes an important contribution. In heaven there can be canon lawyers like Gratian,
as well as civil lawyers like Justinian—but there is no canon
law or civil law in heaven. Neither is any necessary, for heaven
is ruled by the divine Justice itself, symbolized by the Divine
Eagle who speaks in Canto XIX.[90] "The vision that your world
receives," the Eagle explains to the pilgrim from earth,

> can penetrate into Eternal Justice
> no more than eye can the sea.[91]

But in Paradise, as Dante says to the Eagle, this Eternal Justice
is apprehended without a veil.[92] So it is with the divine Justice
underlying civil law as well. Justinian speaks in paradise of
"the true Justice that inspires me [*la viva giustizia che mi
spira*]."[93] But already in the *Inferno*, Dante, in the very first of
the many references of the poem to Florence, has characterized it as a city so filled with envy that "its sack has always
spilled,"[94] pouring out envy and injustice in place of the justice
that had been dominant when "courtesy and valor" prevailed
there and that should still be the glory of its laws.[95] The tragedy
of the Church on earth, which multiplies legislation but smoth-
ers justice, is thrown into the sharpest possible relief by a comparison with the Church in heaven, which celebrates justice,
even the deep and mysterious justice at work in the eternal
damnation of the heathen,[96] and which rewards both Justinian

---

[90]Chierici 1962, 156–158.
[91]*Par*.XIX.58–60.
[92]*Par*.XIX.28–30.
[93]*Par*.VI.88.
[94]*Inf*.VI.49–50.
[95]*Inf*.XVI.67, X.82–87.
[96]*Par*.XIX.70–89.

and Gratian, those codifiers of, as the lawyers put it, *utriusque juris*, "both kinds of law," or, as Dante puts it, "*l'uno e l'altro foro* [one and the other court of law],"[97] with the gift of eternal glory in the presence of Eternal Justice in paradise.

In addition to hierarchy and law, another point both of analogy and of difference between the Church on earth and the Church in heaven as portrayed in the *Paradiso* is the doctrinal theology of the Church. Ever since the thirteenth chapter of 1 Corinthians, and certainly since the *Enchiridion* of Augustine, the three "theological virtues" to which the bulk of the "Secunda Secundae" part of the *Summa Theologica* of Thomas Aquinas was devoted, had been "faith, hope, charity, these three."[98] Faith was represented by the Creed, hope by the Lord's Prayer, charity by the Ten Commandments; and, together, these would form the outline of catechisms throughout the Middle Ages and into the period of the Reformation. Thus, "faith" was seen as comprising the "articles of faith," the *credenda* that had to be believed on pain of excommunication here below and eternal damnation in the life to come. The triad of faith, hope, and charity provides the foundation of Cantos XXIV through XXVI, in which, successively, Saint Peter subjects Dante to an inquisition on faith, Saint James examines him on hope, and Saint John investigates his understanding and practice of charity.

Having already celebrated the theologians in Canto X, Dante has made clear his commitment to the theological enterprise of *fides quaerens intellectum*, "faith in search of understanding." Or, as he puts it here in Canto XXIV,

> it is from this faith that we must reason,
> deducing what we can from syllogisms
> [*da questa credenza si convene sillogizzar*][99]

---

[97] *Par*.X.104.
[98] 1 Cor. 13:13.
[99] *Par*.XXIV.76–77.

—an understanding that went back ultimately to Augustine, but that had been formulated for medieval thought by Anselm of Canterbury. It is Bonaventure who introduces Dante to Anselm.[100] In doing so, however, Bonaventure does not supply the pilgrim with detailed information about the special contribution of Anselm to the enterprise. Nor, for that matter, does Saint Bonaventure speak about Anselm's formulation of the doctrine of the Atonement in his *Cur Deus Homo*. Rather, Beatrice is the one to expound to Dante the Anselmic doctrine of satisfaction through the death of Christ. She does so in the Second Heaven, with great theological erudition and logical insight.[101] Canto XXIV is cast in the form of an academic convocation. Beatrice turns to Saint Peter, asking him to "test this man" on the content of the Faith and to "ask him points light and grave, just as you please."[102] Then the candidate, in turn, gets himself set for the examiner's questions.[103] The examination proceeds from an inquiry into the nature of faith, whose "quiddity" Dante correctly defines on the basis of the New Testament as "the substance of things hoped for and the evidence of things not seen."[104] From there the oral examination goes on, as a medieval inquiry could be expected to do, to the question of proof and authority in theology.[105]

But throughout the examination, in addition to testing the accuracy of Dante's knowledge of the *credenda* and the orthodoxy of his position on them, the examiner is at pains to draw a sharp contrast between this theology of the Church "here" in heaven and much of what goes on in the name of theology down "below" in the Church on earth. When Dante, in response to the question of why the definition of faith derived from the Epistle to the Hebrews speaks of its "substance," replies,

---

[100] *Par*.XII.137.
[101] *Par*.VII.19–120.
[102] *Par*.XXIV.37–38.
[103] *Par*.XXIV.46–51.
[104] *Par*.XXIV.52–66, quoting Heb. 11:1.
[105] *Par*.XXIV.98–102.

> The deep things that on me bestow
> their image here, are hid from sight below,
> so that their being lies in faith alone,[106]

this stress on "faith alone [*sola credenza*]," while it certainly does not mean what the *sola fide* of the Protestant Reformers would mean two centuries or so later, is enough to evoke from Saint Peter the rueful and sardonic comment:

> If all one learns below
> as doctrine were so understood, there would
> be no place for the sophist's cleverness.[107]

For in Dante's paradise there may be canon lawyers, but there is no canon law; heaven, though, does contain both theology and theologians. Yet that is a theology, as Thomas Aquinas would say, *in patria*,[108] of those who have already arrived "in the homeland," where, in Saint Paul's phrase, they know even as also they are known.[109] But the theology for those who are still *in via*, "on the way or on pilgrimage"—or, in the word that Dante puts into the mouth of Peter, "below [*giù*],"[110]—is different not only quantitatively, in that those *in patria* know more things, but qualitatively, in that they know God "face to face." Therefore, it behooves the *theologia viatorum* to be ever conscious of that fundamental distinction between the Church on earth and the Church in heaven, and not to make pretenses about being able to lay claim to a knowledge available only in glory.

In Canto XXIII of the *Paradiso*, after Beatrice, "her face all aflame" and with "gladness" in her eyes, has exclaimed to Dante the pilgrim,

---

[106] *Par.*XXIV.70–74.
[107] *Par.*XXIV.79–81.
[108] *S.T.* IIa IIae.180.7 *ad* 3.
[109] 1 Cor. 13:12.
[110] *Par.*XXIV.80.

> There you see the troops
> of the triumphant Christ![111]

thus pointing beyond herself to the Church, the climax of that vision of the Church Triumphant is the coronation and triumph of the Virgin Mary,[112] the most sublime of the three Eternal Feminines. For, as John D. Sinclair suggests: "the Church Militant centres in Beatrice, the Church Triumphant in the Virgin, 'the rose in which the divine Word was made flesh,' 'the inn of our desire'; and Beatrice is here but an observer, first expectant and eager, then directing Dante's attention. For we are passing from the reflection to the light itself, from the doctrine to the realities of which the doctrine tells." And that, as he goes on to note, takes us to "the cult of the Virgin, which . . . was really the cult of the Incarnation, and Mary, for the worshipper, the peculiar channel and embodiment of grace."[113]

---

[111] *Par.*XXIII.19–24.

[112] *Par.*XXIII.79–129.

[113] Sinclair 1961, 3:340; see also 369.

# FIVE

# Mary as *Nostra Regina*

THE thirteen tercets that open the closing canto of the *Paradiso*, which are addressed to the Blessed Virgin Mary by Bernard of Clairvaux (and in great measure derived from his many writings in praise of Mary),[1] and which begin with the words

> *Vergine madre, figlia del tuo Figlio,*
> *umile e alta più che creatura*
> [Virgin mother, daughter of your Son,
> more humble and sublime than any creature],[2]

must be regarded, whether they be judged by the criteria of piety or by those of poetics, as a high point, probably as *the* high point, in the history of medieval Marian poetry—a genre that would include such masterpieces as the *Stabat Mater Dolorosa* (to which Dante may be alluding both in the *Purgatorio* and in the *Paradiso*),[3] the *Salve Regina* (which Dante quotes in the *Purgatorio*),[4] and the *Regina Coeli* (which Dante quotes in the *Paradiso*,[5] as part of what has been called

---

[1] Barré 1953, 92–113; Graef 1963–1965, 1:235–241.
[2] *Par*.XXXIII.1–2.
[3] *Purg*.XXXIII.6; *Par*.XI.71–72.
[4] *Purg*.VII.82.
[5] *Par*.XXIII.127–129.

the "canto of apotheosis"),[6] as well as the almost countless variations on the theme *Ave maris stella*. As Henry Osborn Taylor has said of this final canto, it is a "prayer so beautiful and so expressive of mediaeval thought and feeling as to the most kind and blessed Lady of Heaven. This prayer or hymn is made of phrases which the mediaeval mind and heart had been recasting and perfecting for centuries. It is almost a great *cento*, like the *Dies Irae*."[7] Within the structure of the *Paradiso*, and perhaps within the structure of the *Divine Comedy* as a whole, this apostrophe to Mary stands as a summation and as a goal of the entire poem. For it is Mary, as the "gentle lady" in heaven, by whose intercession the "stern judgment up above is shattered," who, near the very beginning of the poem, issues the command to Beatrice to go to the assistance of the poet,

> who loves you so
> that—for your sake—he's left the vulgar crowd,

thus setting the whole itinerary of the *Divine Comedy* into motion.[8] And at the very conclusion of the poem, Mary is to Dante not only "Our Lady [*nostra donna*]"[9] but "our Queen [*nostra regina*],"[10] "the Queen of heaven,"[11] and "the Empress [*Agusta*],"[12] the fulfillment of the promise of paradise and the archetype of all who are saved.

Being "more humble and sublime than any creature,"[13] Mary becomes the supreme instance of the counterpoint between the Eternal and the Feminine, between the historical and the allegorical. In her case, the counterpoint is a theme taken explicitly from the New Testament, whose words Dante

---

[6]Masseron 1953, 82.
[7]Taylor 1938, 2:581.
[8]*Inf.*II.95–105.
[9]*Par.*XXI.123.
[10]*Par.*XXXII.104.
[11]*Par.*XXIII.128.
[12]*Par.*XXXII.119.
[13]*Par.*XXXIII.2.

is echoing here. For in the Magnificat (according to the Vulgate) she had sung: "For he hath regarded the humility of his handmaiden; behold, from henceforth all generations shall call me blessed [*Quia respexit humilitatem ancillae suae. Ecce enim ex hoc beatam me dicent omnes generationes*]."[14] Throughout the history of the Church, it had been the task of the theological doctrine of Mary, as well as of the tradition of Marian poetry, to look for formulas that would somehow encompass simultaneously both the humility of her life on earth and the blessedness of her participation in the eternal glory of her Son in heaven. In the theological allegory of his own Marian poetry, Dante found a way to do so that at the same time celebrates the continuity of *nostra regina*, as the supreme Eternal Feminine, with the other two Eternal Feminines of the *Divine Comedy*: Beatrice as *donna mia* and the Church as *bella sposa*.[15]

It is easy for the reader to be caught up by the rhapsodic, almost dithyrambic ecstasy of Bernard's poem and by the vision of a transcendent Virgin Mary that it celebrates, and in the process to forget that for Dante and for Bernard of Clairvaux, as for the entire medieval tradition, Mary stands in continuity with the human race, the same human race to which the poet and his readers belong, and therefore that the glory with which she is crowned is a special form—different in degree, of course, but finally not different in kind—of the glory in which all the saved participate, communicated to her, as to them, by the grace and merit of Christ: she is, in the paradox of the Incarnation, the daughter of her Son, who has redeemed her.[16] Early in the *Paradiso*, in response to Dante's unspoken question about the relative degrees of merit and hence of salvation, Beatrice has to explain:

> Neither the Seraph closest unto God,
> nor Moses, Samuel, nor either John—

---

[14]Luke 1:48.
[15]*Enc.Dant.* 3:835–839.
[16]*Par.*XXXIII.1.

whichever one you will—*not Mary* has,
I say, their place in any other heaven
than that which houses those souls you just saw,
nor will their blessedness last any longer.[17]

Degrees of salvation there are, and therefore circles of paradise, "in ways diverse" and "from stage to stage," as Beatrice has explained to him even earlier.[18] Without such degrees there would not be perfect justice on the basis of merit; and, for that matter, without these degrees of salvation and of damnation there would be no poem. The justice of God is a mystery that remains "past understanding"[19] also when it brings about the damnation of pagans who never had the opportunity to hear the gospel. Nevertheless, those who are destined to dwell eternally in the lower degrees of paradise affirm that "in His will is our peace"; for

every place
in Heaven is in Paradise, though grace
does not rain equally from the High Good,[20]

because these are all degrees of the same heaven and of the one paradise, as Mary is the culminating point of the one humanity, still in the one heaven.

As the culminating point, Mary is the new "Mother of all the living."[21] Therefore, she stands in a typological relation to Eve.[22] This relation of Eve and Mary first appears in an explicit form in the writings of the second-century church father Irenaeus of Lyons. The theme of Mary's continuity with humanity, as expressed in the symbolism of Mary as Second Eve, is, significantly, the theme with which Bernard of Clairvaux begins

---

[17] *Par.*IV.28–33 (italics added).
[18] *Par.*II.118, 122.
[19] *Par.*XIX.98.
[20] *Par.*III.85, 88–90.
[21] Gen. 3:20.
[22] Newman 1987, 89–120.

his discourse about the Virgin Mary in the canto preceding his apostrophe to her:

> The wound that Mary closed and then
> anointed was the wound that Eve—so lovely
> at Mary's feet—had opened and had pierced.[23]

Thus as in the Sentences of the liturgy of the Mass for Lent it was said to be the purpose of Christ's coming that "he [the devil] who by a tree once overcame [that is, by the tree of the knowledge of good and evil in the Garden of Eden] might likewise by a tree be overcome [that is, by the tree of the Cross]," so here he who had overcome through Eve, the original mother of all the living, was likewise overcome in turn through Mary, who is the new mother of all the living.[24] And now, in Bernard's explanation and Dante's vision, Mother Eve is seated at the very feet of Mother Mary—and in a higher place than Rachel or even Beatrice.[25] None of this would comport with the scheme of salvation as Dante is expounding it unless Mary as the Second Eve were genuinely and completely a member of the human race; as Adam had said of the First Eve, "This is now bone of my bones, and flesh of my flesh."[26] And so when Cacciaguida in paradise speaks of how his mother invoked Mary "in pains of birth";[27] or when Buoconte still in purgatory describes having lapsed into a coma after being wounded in battle, just as he "had finished uttering the name of Mary [*nel nome di Maria fini*]";[28] or when Piccarda Donati, after recounting her quite remarkable life story,

> began to sing "*Ave*
> *Maria*" and, while singing, vanished as
> a weighty thing will vanish in deep water[29]—

---

[23]*Par.*XXXII.4–6.
[24]On Eve, see *Enc.Dant.* 2:768–769.
[25]*Par.*XXXII.7–9.
[26]Gen. 2:23.
[27]*Par.*XV.133.
[28]*Purg.*V.101.
[29]*Par.*III.121–123.

the one whom all three are invoking *in extremis* is one who, though their mediatrix, is also their fellow human being, who in fact could not truly be their mediatrix unless she were their fellow human being.

She is, of course, at the same time the personal embodiment of the supreme virtues of which humanity is made capable through the gift of grace: in her, as Bernard says, "is every goodness found in any creature [*quantunque in creatura è di bontate*]."[30] Yet, in this connection there is a curious circumstance in the *Divine Comedy*, and one whose explanation is by no means obvious: much of the most explicit consideration of the specific virtues of Mary appears in the *Purgatorio* rather than here in the *Paradiso*. The hymn of Bernard does laud her as "the noonday torch of charity [*meridiana face di caritate*]" for those already in heaven and as "a living spring of hope [*di speranza fontana vivace*]" for those still on earth.[31] Therefore, she not only manifests great faith, which is implicit throughout,[32] but she is likewise the exemplar of both hope and charity. In short, she embodies all three of the virtues of which Saint Paul speaks.[33] It is on these three virtues that, in Cantos XXIV–XXVI, Dante is examined by the three apostles, or "doves,"[34] Peter, James, and John, a trio who have already been anticipated in the closing cantos of the *Purgatorio*[35] and who form the inner circle of the Twelve.[36] Yet, the specific virtues for which Mary is being singled out in the *Purgatorio*, rather than those which are identified with her in the *Paradiso*, are the ones that stand out. Perhaps part of the reason is

---

[30] *Par.* XXXIII.21.

[31] *Par.* XXXIII.10–12.

[32] So, for example, *Par.* XXXII.37–39, where she would seem to be the supreme example of the faith that is spoken of.

[33] 1 Cor. 13:13.

[34] Bambeck 1979, 147–154.

[35] *Purg.* XXXII.73.

[36] Peter, James, and John are the only ones present at the raising of the daughter of Jairus (Mark 5:37), on the Mount of Transfiguration (Matt. 17:1–9), and in the Garden of Gethsemane (Matt. 26:36–37).

that the souls in paradise are already enjoying the fruits of virtue, which they share (though in lesser measure) with Mary, while those in purgatory, who have still to attain paradise, stand in need of the grace that is merited and communicated through the virtues of Mary, which therefore need to be specified here in more detail.

Thus the attack on "arrogant Christians [*superbi cristian*]" in Canto X of the *Purgatorio* has as its foil the humility of the Virgin Mary, who called herself "the handmaid of God [*ancilla Dei*]."[37] Similarly, when the pilgrim comes to the place where

> the sin of envy
> is scourged within this circle,

what he hears arising from those who are being cleansed of such envy is "the cry of, 'Mary pray for us.' "[38] Further on, as he sees

> people whom the fire of wrath
> had kindled,

they are contrasted with "the gentle manner" of the Virgin's reproof to her twelve-year-old Son when she found him in the temple at Jerusalem.[39] The terrace of those who have been guilty of "sloth and negligence [*negligenza e indugio*]" is one where it is no longer Mary's "gentle manner" but her "haste [*fretta*]" and her zeal that are being celebrated.[40] The sin of avarice, whose "hungering is deep and never-ending," causes its victims here in purgatory to lament, "Sweet Mary [*Dolce Maria*]!"[41] Those "whose appetite was gluttonous" stand in the sharpest possible contrast with Mary, who did not concern herself with satisfying her own hunger.[42] And those who are in

---

[37] *Purg.*X.121, 44.
[38] *Purg.*XIII.37–38, 50.
[39] *Purg.*XV.106, 88–89 (quoting Luke 2:48–49).
[40] *Purg.*XVIII.107, 100.
[41] *Purg.*XX.14, 19.
[42] *Purg.*XXIII.65, XXII.142–144.

purgatory to burn away the fires of lust must cry aloud the words of the Virgin Mary in her chastity.[43] The tour through purgatory thereby becomes at the same time a catalog of the virtues of the Blessed Virgin.

For in Dante's view of the empirical Church and its need for reform, the debates of the thirteenth and fourteenth centuries over poverty and property carried great importance. The discourse of Thomas Aquinas about Francis in Canto XI of the *Paradiso* describes the spiritual marriage between Francis and Lady Poverty, who had been "deprived of her first husband," Christ, and who had thereafter remained without a suitor for "eleven hundred years and more," until the coming of Francis.[44] But one of the questions being debated in the Franciscan controversies over poverty during Dante's time was whether, like Christ, Mary too had taken a vow of absolute poverty, and, if she had, what she had done, for example, with all that gold, frankincense, and myrrh that the Wise Men from the East had brought to her and to her Child. Dante's answer to the question of Mary's poverty seems unequivocal: "Sweet Mary!" Dante hears a voice say in purgatory,

> In that hostel where
> you had set down your holy burden, there
> one can discover just how poor you were.[45]

The chastity of the Virgin Mary, who was (as Bernard says of her in the two opening words of his song) unique among women in being both a virgin and a mother at the same time,[46] is contrasted in the *Purgatorio* not only with "the force of Venus' poison," the extramarital unchastity of others, but even with the marital chastity of virtuous wedlock: "*Virum non cognosco* [I know not a man]," as Mary said, in Latin, to the angel

---

[43] *Purg.*XXV.121–128.
[44] *Par.*XI.58–66.
[45] *Purg.*XX.19–24; Luke 2:7.
[46] *Par.*XXXIII.1.

of the Annunciation.[47] And when Dante confronts in purgatory those souls who had been guilty of the sins of gluttony and drunkenness in this life, he is reminded once more of the contrast with the virtue of Mary, manifested at the wedding feast in Cana of Galilee, and of her role as mediatrix both at Cana and now here in purgatory. As a voice explains,

> Mary's care was for the marriage-
> feast's being seemly and complete, not for
> her mouth (which now would intercede for you),[48]

continuing in heaven the intercession that she had articulated while on earth.

It is likewise in the *Purgatorio* that Dante the poet also first describes the relation Mary bears to the angels. The two guardian angels dressed in green whom Dante the pilgrim sees, with their flaming swords shortened but their faces blinding for sheer brilliance, "both come from Mary's bosom," Sordello tells him,

> to serve as the custodians of the valley
> against the serpent that will soon appear.[49]

This conjunction of Mary and the serpent seems to be a typological fulfillment of the promise of the protevangelium in the story of the Fall, according to which God said to the serpent in the Garden of Eden: "And I will put enmity between thee and the woman, and between thy seed and her seed; *she* shall bruise thy head, and thou shalt bruise *her* heel."[50] Or so, at any rate, it read in the Vulgate, which had translated the personal pronoun as feminine: "*ipsa* conteret caput tuum." By agreeing, in her words to the angel, "Be it done to me according

---

[47] *Purg.*XXV.128–135, quoting Luke 1:34.
[48] *Purg.*XXII.142–144, citing John 2:3.
[49] *Purg.*VIII.25–39.
[50] Gen. 3:15.

to thy word [*Fiat mihi secundum verbum tuum*]," to accept the commission of God to become the mother of the Savior, Mary, the *ancilla* or handmaid of the Lord,[51] was seen as having carried out that divine promise (or, from the serpent's point of view, that divine threat) and thereby as having turned the "key"[52] to open the door of the supreme love of God for a fallen humanity.

The other reference in the *Purgatorio* to Mary's relation with the angels appears two cantos later. The pilgrim is contemplating an amazingly beautiful wall of white marble, adorned with carvings that put to shame not only the greatest of human sculptors but nature herself.[53] Carved on the marble wall is the figure of the angel Gabriel, the angel of the Annunciation to Mary:

> The angel who reached earth with the decree
> of that peace which, for many years, had been
> invoked with tears, the peace that opened Heaven
> after long interdict, appeared before us,
> his gracious action carved with such precision—
> he did not seem to be a silent image.
> One would have sworn that he was saying, "*Ave*";
> for in that scene there was the effigy
> of one who turned the key that had unlocked
> the highest love; and in her stance there were
> impressed these words, "*Ecce ancilla Dei*,"
> precisely like a figure stamped in wax.[54]

Already in purgatory, therefore, the divinely decreed mission of the Virgin Mary to "turn the key" and become the human means for the Incarnation and thereby for salvation is being announced to the souls that await release into paradise; and already in purgatory the angels are making it evident that they

---

[51] Luke 1:38.
[52] *Purg.* X.42.
[53] *Purg.* X.31–33.
[54] *Purg.* X.34–45.

stand ready to serve her and, through her, both her divine Son and the humanity he came to save.

It is, nevertheless, in paradise that the special relation between Mary and the angels is disclosed in all its glory. Once again, the angel Gabriel,

> the angelic love who had descended
> earlier, now spread his wings before her,
> singing *"Ave Maria, gratia plena."*[55]

But this time it is not, as it was in purgatory, in a mere physical representation on cold marble, which may be beautiful but is not alive, but in the spiritual reality of heaven itself that Gabriel continues forever the ·salutation with which the history of salvation began[56] (and from which, rather than from the Nativity of Christ itself, Dante, who follows the Florentine custom, dates the beginning of the new era through the Incarnation)[57]—not any longer in the "modest voice" of his original greeting,[58] but in full-throated praise. In his salutation and praise he is joined by all the angelic hosts of heaven. Dante the pilgrim saw and heard the heavenly "brightnesses [*candori*]" as they expressed "the deep affection each possessed for Mary" and as they sang the *Regina Coeli* so sweetly that, Dante the poet adds, "my delight in that has never left" even now as he writes.[59] It is a song in praise of Mary in which the angels are joined by the Church Triumphant of the saved who have already come to paradise.[60] As "the greatest flame [*lo maggior foco*],"[61] Mary, "Lady of Heaven [*donna del ciel*]," is the object of this angelic paean:

---

[55] *Par.* XXXII.94–96.
[56] *Par.* XVI.34.
[57] *Par.* XVI.34–39.
[58] *Par.* XIV.36.
[59] *Par.* XXIII.124–129.
[60] *Par.* XXIII.130–132.
[61] *Par.* XXIII.90.

> I am angelic love who wheel around
> that high gladness inspired by the womb
> that was the dwelling place of our Desire;
> so shall I circle, Lady of Heaven, until
> you, following your Son, have made that sphere
> supreme, still more divine by entering it.[62]

This "ineffable vision,"[63] which attributes to Mary the ability to make the glories of the supreme sphere of heaven "still more [*dia più*]" through her presence, prepares Dante for the sublimely ineffable vision of Mary and the angels that will come to him as the occasion for Bernard's discourse about the Blessed Virgin.

It is that vision which is described in the concluding tercets of Canto XXXI of the *Paradiso*. As his awe has deepened, the pilgrim has been reluctant to contemplate the full power and glory before him. Therefore, "son of grace" that he is, he must be admonished:

> You will not come to know this joyous state
> if your eyes only look down at the base;
> but look upon the circles, look at those
> that sit in a position more remote,
> until you see upon her seat the Queen
> to whom this realm is subject and devoted
> [*la regina cui questo regno è suddito e devoto*].[64]

The souls of the saints who have already come to heaven, including in particular "the Hebrew women,"[65] are part of the celestial realm, and Mary is their archetype. But the angels, those dread and powerful spirits who do God's bidding day and night, have been its citizens all along, and there they have remained even after their rebellious fellow angels have been

---

[62]*Par.*XXIII.103–108.
[63]Masseron 1953, 82–83.
[64]*Par.*XXXI.112–117.
[65]Di Scipio 1984, 57–85.

cast into hell, where, as the pilgrim learned, the demons have now become as foul as they once were fair.[66] And since Mary is indeed the "Queen of heaven [*Regina coeli*]," she is "Queen of angels," too.

Lifting his eyes in response to the admonition, the "son of grace," in language reminiscent of the apocalyptic visions of Ezekiel, Daniel, and Saint John the Divine,

> . . . as, at morning,
> the eastern side of the horizon shows
> more splendor than the side where the sun sets,
> so, as if climbing with my eyes from valley
> to summit, saw one part of the farthest
> rank of the Rose more bright than all the rest.[67]

Before the transcendent light of the glorified queen of heaven, the angels gather—not an indiscriminate mob, but as distinct individuals, since, as Thomas Aquinas taught, "it is impossible for two angels to be of one species," but each had to be a species unto itself.[68] The poet describes what he saw:

> I saw, around that midpoint, festive angels—
> more than a thousand—with their wings outspread;
> each was distinct in splendor and in skill.[69]

The "midpoint" and the object of their sportive celebration is the ineffable beauty of Mary, who rules over a realm in which both saints and angels have their place:

> And there I saw a loveliness that when
> it smiled at the angelic songs and games
> made glad the eyes of all the other saints.

---

[66] *Inf.* XXXIV.34.
[67] *Par.* XXXI.118–123.
[68] *S.T.* I.50.4.
[69] *Par.* XXXI.130–132.

Here it becomes the task of poetic language about transcendent reality not to describe the object, but to describe its own incapacity to describe the object:

> And even if my speech were rich as my
> imagination is, I should not try
> to tell the very least of her delights.[70]

That sentence needs to be parsed with some care. As his treatises on literature and language attest, Dante was honest enough to know that he had a skill with words, and it would have been the most hypocritical kind of false modesty for him to pretend otherwise. Moreover, here he recognizes in himself a "wealth of imaginative power [*divizia ad imaginar*]," and he finds that it in turn far exceeds all of this verbal power. Yet even if it did not, he says, if word could truly be matched to imagination in some simple one-to-one correlation, that would be inadequate for describing Mary—indeed, inadequate for describing not just her regal and transcendent position in the cosmos, but "the very least of her delights [*lo minimo di sua delizia*]."

It would be easy to read all of this extravagant language about the Virgin Mary as what Protestant polemics against medieval Catholicism came to call "Mariolatry."[71] It would be easy, but it would be superficial and mistaken. For, to quote again from Henry Osborn Taylor, "One may say that the *Commedia* begins and ends with the Virgin. It was she who sent Beatrice into the gates of Hell to move Virgil—meaning human reason—to go to Dante's aid. The prayer which obtains her benediction, and the vision following, close the *Paradiso*." But, he warns, "no more with Dante than with other mediaeval men is she the end of worship and devotion. Her eyes are turned to God. So are those of Beatrice, of Rachel, and of all the saints in Paradise."[72] Mary could not be the archetype of the saved unless she herself had been saved. She had been

---

[70] *Par.* XXXI.133–138.
[71] *OED* 6–II:165.
[72] Taylor 1938, 2:581–582.

saved in a special manner, as by now almost all the theologians of the Church affirmed, although it would not finally become official and binding until 1854—that is, by being preserved from original sin, rather than, as everyone else was, rescued from it—but saved by the same divine grace and through the same divine Redeemer as the rest of humanity. Dante's attitude toward this explanation of Mary's holiness is not altogether clear, but in Canto XIII he has Thomas Aquinas declare:

> I do approve of the opinion
> you hold, that human nature never was
> nor shall be what it was in those two persons,

namely, in Adam and in Christ.[73] This does seem to justify the conclusion drawn by Alexandre Masseron: "Dante affirms that Christ and Adam are the only ones who were created perfect," the explicit position of Bernard of Clairvaux, who rejected the doctrine of the Immaculate Conception.[74] Such was as well the teaching of Saint Thomas.[75] That, in turn, makes it necessary to consider the question of the relation of Mary to Christ in Dante's theology.[76]

Perhaps the most trenchant summary of it comes near the end of the poem, when Bernard of Clairvaux instructs Dante (once again, as throughout the *Divine Comedy*, rhyming the name Cristo only with itself):

> Look now upon the face that is most like
> the face of Christ, for only through its brightness
> can you prepare your vision to see Him
> [*Riguarda omai ne la faccia che a Cristo
> più si somiglia, ché la sua chiarezza
> sola ti può disporre a veder Cristo*].[77]

---

[73] *Par.* XIII.85–87.

[74] Masseron 1953, 139–141.

[75] *S.T.* III.27.2.

[76] The entire chapter "The Mother of God" in Newman 1987, 156–195, bears upon the subject of the present chapter.

[77] *Par.* XXXII.85–87.

This privilege of beholding Mary, which has been granted in special measure to Bernard and which Dante then proceeds to share with Bernard, is a transforming vision and quite literally an indescribable one. Yet it remains a vision that prepares for an infinitely grander vision and that points beyond itself to the vision of Christ as "the exalted Son of God and of Mary [*l'alto Filio di Dio e di Maria*]," [78] and to the beatific vision of God as the Trinity of Father, Son, and Holy Spirit. It has been the historic mission of the Virgin Mary to make this vision and revelation of the Holy Trinity possible for humanity. For as Virgil, who by now has picked up more than a smattering of knowledge about the Trinitarian faith of Catholic Christendom (and about Scholastic theology), warns Dante already in purgatory:

> Foolish is he who hopes our intellect
> can reach the end of that unending road
> only one Substance in three Persons follows.
> Confine yourselves, o humans, to the *quia*;
> had you been able to see all, there would
> have been no need for Mary to give birth— [79]

thereby confessing the doctrine of the Trinity, the doctrine of the relation between reason and revelation, and (at least implicitly) the doctrine of the Virgin Birth, each of them in impeccably orthodox language.

Whatever may be Dante's doctrine about the special privilege of the Immaculate Conception at the beginning of the life of the Blessed Virgin, he clearly does teach, as does Bernard, that at the end of her life Mary was granted the privilege of the Assumption, through the grace of Christ. Therefore, Saint John explains very carefully concerning himself that (*pace* some legends about him) he has not received this privilege of being assumed into heaven:

---

[78] *Par.* XXIII.136–137.
[79] *Purg.* III.34–39.

> On earth my body now is earth and shall
> be there together with the rest until
> our number equals the eternal purpose.

But then John adds the significant stipulation, speaking of Mary and of Christ:

> Only those two lights that ascended wear
> their double garment in this blessed cloister,[80]

the "double garment" being the body and the soul, not only the soul. The two are Christ (through the Ascension narrated in the New Testament and confessed in the Creed) and then Mary (through the Assumption celebrated throughout the liturgy of the medieval Church but not officially promulgated as dogma until 1950). When Dante, bidden by Beatrice, lifts his eyes to behold Mary in heaven as

> the Rose in which the Word of God became
> flesh,[81]

he celebrates the Ascension of Christ as an event intended "to grant scope to the eyes there that had not strength for Thee," and immediately goes on to recognize that through her bodily Assumption into heaven Mary shared in that exaltation, becoming not only "the fair flower which I always invoke morning and evening" on earth, but "the greatest of the fires" in the empyrean.[82] Therefore, it is to Mary assumed into heaven that Bernard addresses his petition on Dante's behalf, to "curb his mortal passions" and to "disperse all the clouds of his mortality," so that Dante might receive the vision of the "Eternal Light" and so that "the Highest Joy might be his to see."[83]

---

[80] *Par.* XXV.127–128.
[81] *Par.* XXIII.73–74.
[82] *Par.* XXIII.86–90.
[83] *Par.* XXXIII.31–43.

Seeing that "Eternal Light" is the content of the vision of God. And in the final hundred lines of the final canto of the *Paradiso*, Dante celebrates the vision of the Trinity of three divine Persons in one divine Substance:

> In the deep and bright
> essence of that exalted Light, three circles
> appeared to me; they had three different colors,
> but all of them were of the same dimension;
> one circle seemed reflected by the second,
> as rainbow is by rainbow, and the third
> seemed fire breathed equally by those two circles.[84]

Therefore, it must not be forgotten that a canto opening with the celebration of the Virgin Mary by Bernard of Clairvaux goes on—through her and not around her, but nevertheless beyond her—to the celebration of the Eternal Light and Eternal "Love that moves the sun and the other stars,"[85] including Mary as the sun from which "the morning star draws beauty"[86] and Mary as *stella maris*, the star of the sea and the queen of heaven. Hence there is not, in those final hundred lines, a single explicit reference to her; or perhaps it is all a reference to her, as the fellow creature (so Bernard explicitly describes her)[87] who has pioneered in this vision. And that would be in keeping with her role throughout the poem, as the Heavenly Muse whose intervention, described by Beatrice already in Canto II of the *Inferno*,[88] has made it all possible. Thus "Maria" was for Dante

> the name of that fair flower which I always
> invoke, at morning and at evening;[89]

---

[84] *Par.* XXXIII.115–120.
[85] *Par.* XXXIII.145.
[86] *Par.* XXXII.107–108.
[87] *Par.* XXXIII.21.
[88] *Inf.* II.85–114.
[89] *Par.* XXIII.88–89.

and he went on invoking it throughout the *Comedy*, singing the *Salve Regina* to her already while traveling through purgatory[90] but becoming her most eloquent troubadour in the *Paradiso*, above all in its final canto. By extension, moreover, that role—transcendent, but, as we have seen, also self-transcending—is the role of all three of Dante's Eternal Feminines, each of whom, in ascending order, points beyond herself to the other two, but all of whom point beyond themselves to Christ and the Holy Trinity.

––––––––––
[90] *Purg*.VII.82.

# Epilogue: Wisdom
## as *Sophia* and *Sapienza*

AMONG the Eternal Feminines in the language of the Christian tradition to which Dante was heir, in addition to those that have been examined in the preceding chapters, there was perhaps none with so rich and varied a history, and with so promising a set of implications, as *Sophia*, the personification of Wisdom.[1] Despite its having been appropriated by Gnosticism as a name for one of the divine aeons,[2] it was central to the orthodox Greek church fathers in their exposition of the doctrine of the Trinity. Indeed, the words of Wisdom in the Book of Proverbs—beginning (in the Greek of the Septuagint) with the declaration, so vexing for Trinitarian orthodoxy, "The Lord created me [ἔκτισέ με] the beginning of his ways for his works. I was set up from everlasting, from the beginning, or ever the earth was"[3]—were at least part of the background for the words of the prologue to the Gospel according to Saint John: "In the beginning was the Word, and the Word was with God, and the Word was God. The same was in the beginning with God. All things were made by him; and without him was not any thing made that was made."[4] Therefore, the exegesis

---

[1]Lampe 1961, 1244–1246, s.v. "σοφία," cites literally hundreds of passages from the Greek church fathers; of particular interest are those grouped under the headings "in relation to [the] Holy Ghost" and "of [the] Son."

[2]As reported by Irenaeus *Against Heresies* I.i.7.

[3]Prov. 8:22–31.

[4]John 1:1–3.

of this discourse by Sophia in the eighth chapter of the Book of Proverbs occupied no less prominent a place in the development of Trinitarian theology than did the exegesis of the words of Saint John. As the divine patron of the greatest church in Christendom, Hagia Sophia in Constantinople, Sophia has remained a central theme in the vocabulary of Eastern Christianity, both Greek and Slavic, into the twentieth century.[5] Recent studies of medieval mysticism have shown, moreover, that Sophia continued, despite its identification with the *Logos* as the second person of the Trinity incarnate in the man Jesus Christ, to carry feminine connotations as *creatrix* and as *anima mundi* also in the usage of the Latin West.[6] This was at least partly because she was identified not only as the second person of the Trinity or as the third person of the Trinity, but sometimes also as the Blessed Virgin Mary.

Dante accorded a prominent place to Wisdom in his thought.[7] After denouncing in the *Inferno* the false wisdom of Simon Magus and his "sad disciples," the poet immediately goes on to praise the authentic *Somma Sapienza*:

> O Highest Wisdom, how much art you show
> in heaven, earth, and this sad world below,
> how just your power is when it allots![8]

In the *Paradiso*, on the other hand, after Dante has Saint Thomas Aquinas present his catalog of the "many lights, alive, most bright,"[9] those whose lives were devoted to the authentic theological wisdom of which the heresy of Simon Magus is a caricature (including, rather incongruously, Siger of Brabant), he significantly "calls our attention to Christ, the second person of the Trinity and the exemplar of all wisdom—*Somma Sapienza.*"[10] He also knew the passage from the Book of Prov-

---

[5] Newman 1978.
[6] Newman 1987, 64–71.
[7] Alverny 1965; *Enc.Dant.* 5:27–30.
[8] *Inf.*XIX.10–12.
[9] *Par.*X.64.
[10] Freccero 1986, 237.

erbs, albeit in the Vulgate rendition: "Dominus possedit me in initio viarum suarum, antequam quidquam faceret a principio; ab aeterno ordinata sum et ex antiquis, antequam terra fieret." He quotes it in the *Convivio*, but he identifies the "donna gentile" who speaks these words as Philosophy.[11] Gilson's comment on this exegesis of Proverbs 8 deserves to be quoted in full:

> "E però ultimamente dico che *da eterno*, cioè etternamente, *fu ordinata* (*sc.* questa donna gentile) ne la mente di Dio in testimonio de la fede a coloro che in questo tempo vivono" (*Convivio*, III, 7). Dante is here alluding to *Prov.*, VIII, 23: "Ab aeterno ordinata sum ex antiquis antequam terra fieret"; but in thus applying to philosophic wisdom that which all the theologians of his time applied to the eternal Wisdom, which is the Word, Dante was certainly adopting an entirely personal attitude to the question.[12]

Gilson is using this passage from the *Convivio* to refute any simplistic identification of Dante's outlook with that of Thomas Aquinas, but in so doing he also suggests why Wisdom as Sapienza does not in Dante's usage assume the proportions of Wisdom as Sophia in the Greek Christian tradition, nor even in the Latin Christian tradition, even though "Dante thinks of all knowledge in terms of Christ, the Wisdom of God."[13]

This explanation also helps to illumine the place occupied in the *Divine Comedy* by Wisdom as Sapienza, and by Solomon as its principal biblical expositor. As Dante's Thomas Aquinas says, pointing to him in that same Canto X of the *Paradiso*,

> there is the lofty mind where such profound
> wisdom was placed that, if the truth be true,
> no other ever rose with so much vision.[14]

---

[11] *Conv.*III.7.
[12] Gilson 1949, 118, n.1.
[13] Ralphs 1959, 13.
[14] *Par.*X.112–114.

Solomon lived before the Incarnation, but he knew the divine Wisdom. Moreover, he was not a Scholastic philosopher, but

> it was as a king that he had asked
> for wisdom that would serve his royal task—
> and not to know the number of the angels
> on high, or, if combined with a contingent,
> *necesse* ever can produce *necesse*,
> or *si est dare primum motum esse*,
> or if, within a semicircle, one
> can draw a triangle with no right angle:

he asked for "matchless vision," that is, "kingly prudence [*regal prudenza*]," rather than for answers to all those speculative questions that seem so troubling to Scholastic philosophy (but that Dante clearly regards as trivial).[15] These words in praise of King Solomon, then, are simultaneously a paean to Wisdom and a polemic against wisdom falsely so called.

Taken together with the warning against human presumption and the inordinate desire for knowledge and power with which the *Paradiso* opens—

> Nearing its desired end,
> our intellect sinks into an abyss
> so deep that memory fails to follow it[16]—

this vision of Solomon the Wise in Canto XIII of the *Paradiso* almost unavoidably calls to mind one of the most poignant scenes in all of Dante's *Divine Comedy* (second only to the pathos-filled depiction of Paolo and Francesca in Canto V of the *Inferno*): the appearance of Ulysses in Canto XXVI of the *Inferno*. The sin for which Ulysses has been condemned to eternal punishment is expressed in his words to his men (for which there is no real source in Homer, whose *Odyssey* Dante, in any case, knew only at second hand):[17]

---

[15] *Par.*XIII.94–105.

[16] *Par.*I.8–9.

[17] As Toynbee 1965, 66, points out, in the *Vita Nuova* Dante "quotes Homer twice," but never directly.

> ... You must not deny
> experience of that which lies beyond
> the sun, and of the world that is unpeopled.
> Consider well the seed that gave you birth:
> you were not made to live your lives as brutes,
> but to be followers of worth and knowledge.[18]

This is the sin that John D. Sinclair, commenting on this passage from the *Inferno*, defines as "an eternal and insatiable human hunger and quest after knowledge of the world," a sin that Dante knew at first hand; for, in the words Sinclair quotes from Benedetto Croce, "No one of his age was more deeply moved than Dante by the passion to know all that is knowable, and nowhere else has he given such noble expression to that noble passion as in the great figure of Ulysses."[19]

Yet, earlier in the *Inferno*, in Canto IV, Dante has been led to view quite another scene, one that must be described as cosy—cosy, at any rate, for hell—when he sees "the master of them that know [*'l maestro di color che sanno*]," seated among the philosophers.[20] And that "master of them that know" is, of course, Aristotle, to whom his own teachers and all the philosophers of antiquity, catalogued here by Dante, are now in the life to come obliged to bow down, rather like the sons of Jacob before their brother Joseph in his dream of the sheaves.[21] To complement Dante's picture of the master of knowledge, moreover, it should be noted that Aristotle's most famous pupil, the master of power, is also in hell: the name of Alexander the Great is listed as the very first among "the tyrants who plunged their hands in blood and plundering" and who now "lament their ruthless crimes [*si piangon li spietati danni*]."[22] At least two of the many other masters of power who appear in the *Divine Comedy* deserve special comment. The first of

---

[18] *Inf.* XXVI.115–119.
[19] Sinclair 1961, 1:331.
[20] *Inf.* IV.130–135.
[21] Cf. Gen. 37:7.
[22] *Inf.* XII.104–107.

the repeated denunciations of Pope Boniface VIII, which appears in Canto VI of the *Inferno*, refers to his having abused his "power [*forza*]," [23] and later, in Canto XIX, he is described as having employed cunning to violate *la bella donna*, the Church. [24] On the other hand, power is not *eo ipso* evil. The Emperor Justinian is said by Beatrice to be "like a god," [25] and he is the only figure to be given an entire canto for his speech, Canto VI of the *Paradiso*, to discourse on the meaning of "governing the world beneath the shadow of sacred wings." [26] In that discourse, Justinian presents a capsule history of the Roman Empire from pagan through Christian times. The message of his narrative of the history of Rome, according to Beatrice, is that "just vengeance can deserve just punishment" in the death of Christ at the hands of Roman power, which was therefore not a lynching but a legal execution. [27]

From those several vignettes in the *Divine Comedy* of Dante, it would appear that as a student of Wisdom he was profoundly aware of the paradox of knowledge and power, as well as of the ambiguity of both. It is intelligence and the capacity for knowledge that set the human creature apart from other beings; what Beatrice "imparadises" is "my mind [*la mia mente*]." [28] Indeed, Dante's Ulysses seems to be echoing the medieval doctrine of the *imago Dei* when he urges his followers not to *viver come bruti*, [29] but to be true to the noblest that the Creator has implanted in them. At the same time, Ulysses has been guilty of an intellectual *hybris* for presuming (in the lines of Tennyson's "Ulysses," which have clearly been taken from Dante)

---

[23] *Inf.*VI.69.
[24] *Inf.*XIX.55–57.
[25] *Par.*V.123.
[26] *Par.*VI.7–8.
[27] *Par.*VII.20–21.
[28] *Par.*XXVIII.3.
[29] *Inf.*XXVI.119.

to follow knowledge like a sinking star,
*beyond* the utmost bound of human thought.[30]

For Aristotle to be the master of those who know, therefore, is
a good thing, a faithful actualization of the human potential (to
use a basic Aristotelian distinction), while for Ulysses it is a
bad thing to go "beyond the utmost bound of human thought."
Similarly, the *forza* of Pope Boniface is evil, bringing the punishment of eternal damnation upon the successor of Saint
Peter for having (in the words of Saint Peter himself) made his
burial ground a sewer.[31] By contrast, the heavenly form who
declares, "Caesar I was and am Justinian,"[32] and who wielded
all but absolute power while on earth as emperor of the Ro-
mans, is, now that he has been purged of his Christological
heresy, a full-fledged saint in paradise. Wherein then, according to Dante, lies the difference between knowledge and
knowledge, between power and power? Therefore, what is the
relation between knowledge and power? And, ultimately, what
is the relation of Wisdom as Sapienza to both of these?

Any answer to these questions must begin with knowledge
and with the "master of them that know." At the heart of
the theory of knowledge set forth by the Aristotelians of the
Middle Ages, whether Jewish or Muslim or Christian, is the
acknowledgment of the finiteness, and therefore of the limita-
tion, of human knowledge. Etienne Gilson summarized this
acknowledgment:

> After affirming that God is this and that, one must presently add
> that He is neither this nor that, and finally conclude that He is
> no one of the things that are because He is beyond them all.
> Even in the theology of Thomas Aquinas, wherein God is iden-
> tified with the pure act of being, it is specified that, although it
> be certainly true to say of God that He is, we do not know the

---

[30]Alfred Lord Tennyson, "Ulysses" 31–32 (italics added).
[31]*Par.*XXVII.23–24.
[32]*Par.*VI.10.

meaning of the verb *is* when applied to God. In another passage, as if afraid to let men imagine themselves endowed with a positive knowledge of God, Thomas bluntly states that "neither the Catholic nor the Pagan knows the very nature of God as it is in itself."[33]

And for the formulation of that insight, Thomas Aquinas as well as Dante drew upon both the Judeo-Christian tradition—above all, the word of the Nameless God to Moses from the burning bush in Exodus 3:14, "I am who I am"[34]—and the philosophy of the "master of them that know," the metaphysics of Aristotle. Aristotle's knowledge, pagan in origin though it was, was laudable because he had (except for his regrettable doctrine of the eternity of the world)[35] striven to confine himself to what was knowable within the limits of created human—and, for that matter, created angelic—existence, recognizing that reason was not enough to "reach the end of that unending road."[36] And for that he was, as the *Paradiso* also calls him, " 'l maestro vostro."[37]

The sin of Ulysses, by contrast, and for Dante and Aquinas as Augustinians the sin of Adam and of Satan before Ulysses,[38] consisted in the distortion of that laudable desire for knowledge and excellence, or according to the definitional phrase of Thomas Aquinas, in "the inordinate desire to excel" through an excess of knowing.[39] That was, according to a tradition of the exegesis of Genesis going back to Augustine and earlier, the doctrine taught by the symbol of the "tree of the knowledge of good and evil" in the Garden of Eden: not that it was sinful to know the difference between good and evil, but that the desire to know the Ultimate Mystery was a refusal to accept

---

[33] Gilson 1957, 144–145.
[34] *Par.*XXIV.136.
[35] McKeon 1939, 206–231.
[36] *Purg.*III.34–44.
[37] *Par.*VIII.120.
[38] *Purg.*XXXIII.34–63.
[39] *S.T.*Ia IIae.84.2.

the full implication of one's own humanity. Here the deepest teaching of Catholic orthodoxy and the honest skepticism of Greek and Roman unbelief just touched, though rather uneasily, in the recognition that there remained a realm of being beyond human penetration; where they differed, to be sure, was over the affirmation of the reality of that realm of being. "Agnosticism" was the term that Julian Huxley coined for it in the Darwinist controversies at the end of the nineteenth century; but, long before Huxley (or Darwin), "apophaticism" was a term for the insight that knowledge both began and ended with an awareness of the limitations of knowledge—and that then it continued with the fullest possible exploitation of all the capacity that lay within those limitations. 'Απόφασις is the Greek word for negation; and "apophatic thought" affirms by means of negation, it respects the limits of knowledge in order thereby to know as it would not and could not know if it ignored those limits.[40]

There is a similar paradox in the medieval understanding of power, as Justinian's speech in Canto VI of the *Paradiso*, at once so historically objective and so utterly subjective, amply demonstrates. In Dante's eyes there were good political as well as theological reasons to explain the prominent position of Justinian in his narrative, far exceeding that of Constantine or Charlemagne or any other medieval Western emperor. He had repented of his error in adhering, for a while, to the teaching that in the divine-human person of Jesus Christ there was only a single will, a position that was condemned by the Church because it destroyed the link between the will of the man Jesus and the will of the humanity he had come to redeem; for this repentance Justinian was to be praised, especially because it did not represent the kind of capitulation to clericalism that had been the outcome of the encounter between Justinian's predecessor, Emperor Theodosius, and Saint Ambrose, bishop of Milan (who does not even appear in the *Paradiso*). As that difference suggests, moreover, the arrange-

---

[40]Lampe 1961, 219.

ment of church-state relations in Justinian's Byzantine Empire came closer than the Western medieval models to Dante's own ideal of how the temporal power of the empire and the spiritual power of the Church and papacy were to be coordinated. Although he introduces his discussion of it in the *De Monarchia* with a rather noncommittal "There are those who still say [*Dicunt adhuc quidam*],"[41] Dante's principal attack on the Donation of Constantine is not the question of its historical authenticity. Rather, Dante maintains that in committing "the evil that derives from his good act" the first Christian emperor had no right to cede power, authority, and territory to the papacy (although Constantine personally had been saved),[42] and he praises Justinian for having avoided any such blunder. On both these grounds, then, Justinian stands as the embodiment of the continuity of the Roman-Christian Empire, "the Rome in which Christ is Roman," as Beatrice says, referring to paradise.[43] But his unforgettable historical achievement was to be found in the service he performed for the codification of the law, and in the corresponding place that law occupied in his exercise of political, and even of military, power; it is above all that achievement for which Dante celebrates him here in the *Paradiso*.

That schema of the difference between the legitimate and the illegitimate exercise of power, and of the corresponding difference between the legitimate and the illegitimate pursuit of knowledge, is also a key to Dante's conceptualization of the relation between knowledge and power. But for that relation, a third concept must be introduced alongside knowledge and power.[44] That concept is wisdom, what Dante in the *Convivio* calls "the beauty [*bellezza*]" of wisdom.[45] More than either knowledge or power, the concept of Wisdom owed an equal debt to the Greek and to the Judeo-Christian sources of medie-

---

[41] *Mon.*III.10.

[42] *Par.*XX.55–60.

[43] *Purg.*XXXII.102.

[44] Cosmo 1936, 190–203.

[45] *Conv.*III.8.

val culture. Augustine, who had plenty to say throughout his works about knowledge and, especially in the *City of God*, about power, devoted special attention to the relation between power and wisdom, largely of course because of the conjunction of these two terms as titles for Christ in the New Testament.[46] That is as well the relation between power and wisdom in Christ to which Beatrice alludes on the basis of the same passage from Saint Paul, addressing Dante the pilgrim as they enter the Eighth Heaven:

> What overwhelms you is a Power
> against which nothing can defend itself.
> This is the Wisdom and the Potency [*la Sapienza e la Possanza*]
> that opened roads between the earth and Heaven,
> the paths for which desire had long since waited.[47]

But Dante's direct source for the understanding of the nature of wisdom, and hence of the relation between wisdom, knowledge, and power, is, as we noted earlier, almost certainly Boethius's *Consolation of Philosophy*. In Book I of the *Consolation* Boethius has occasion, quoting Plato, to reflect on the relation of knowledge, wisdom, and power. Sitting in prison, he addresses these words to Lady Philosophy:

> Is this the library which thou thyself hadst chosen to sit in at my house, in which thou has oftentimes discoursed with me of the *knowledge* of divine and human things? . . . But thou didst decree that sentence by the mouth of Plato: That *commonwealths* should be happy if either the students of *wisdom* did govern them, or those which were appointed to govern them would give themselves to the study of *wisdom*.[48]

Most of the remainder of the *Consolation* is given over to the knowledge of what true wisdom is and of how, even in prison

---

[46] Augustine *On the Trinity* VI and VII, in explanation of 1 Cor. 1:24.
[47] *Par*.XXIII.35–39.
[48] *Cons*.I.pr.4.3–5, quoting Plato *Republic* V.473 (italics added).

and stripped of his political power, Boethius can find it. It was
a lesson that Dante the political exile had to learn the hard
way. And that was why Aristotle could be "master of them that
know." His *Politics* had described, better than any Christian
book except perhaps Augustine's *City of God*, the limits that
law and justice placed upon the exercise of power; his *Physics*
and *Metaphysics* had pushed human knowledge to its limits
but had, by and large, respected those limits; and his *Ethics*
had shown how wisdom was to be applied to the concrete
decisions of human existence. Thus in relation both to knowledge and to power, the *bellezza de la Sapienza* found a
spokesman in Aristotle—and in Dante Alighieri.

The primacy of wisdom is evident throughout the *Divine
Comedy*. The portal of hell bears the Trinitarian inscription:

> My Maker was Divine Authority,
> The Highest Wisdom, and the Primal Love
> [*Fecemi la Divina Podestate,*
> *La Somma Sapienza e 'l Primo Amore*],[49]

but it is especially in the Paradiso that it becomes a leitmotiv.
When the poet, at the beginning of Canto II, addresses those

> other few who turned your minds in time
> unto the bread of angels, which provides
> men here with life—but hungering for more— [50]

he is referring to heavenly Wisdom, of which his readers have
had at least a "foretaste." [51] Later in the *Paradiso* he calls it "the
true manna," as in the *Purgatorio* he has spoken of it as "the
daily manna." [52] Similarly, "the truth beyond whose boundary
no truth lies" [53] is not mere knowledge, but wisdom, just as the

---

[49] *Inf*.III.5–6.
[50] *Par*.II.10–12.
[51] *Par*.X.23.
[52] *Par*.XII.84; *Purg*.XI.13.
[53] *Par*.IV.126–127.

"perfected vision" of "the never-ending light" granted to Beatrice[54] is a participation in divine Wisdom, conferred upon
"His fourth family" through the mystery of the Holy Trinity.[55]
*Sapienza* is the special mark of Saint Dominic.[56] It is likewise
from the opening words of the Book of Wisdom that the elabo-
rate vision of Canto XVIII is derived: *"Diligite iustitiam, qui
iudicatis terram* [Love justice, all ye who judge the earth]."[57]
And the prayer of Beatrice for Dante, when it speaks of "that
Source which his thought and longing seek,"[58] is once again a
prayer for wisdom. Thus, although she cannot be said to
qualify for an equal position alongside Beatrice, the Church,
and Mary in the *Paradiso*, Wisdom as Sapienza, too, does deserve to be called an Eternal Feminine.

---

[54] *Par*.V.5, 8.
[55] *Par*.X.49–51.
[56] *Par*.XI.38.
[57] *Par*.XVIII.91–93.
[58] *Par*.XXIV.9.

# Bibliography

Alverny, Marie-Thérèse d'. "Note sur Dante et la Sagesse." *Revue des Etudes Italiennes* 11 (1965):5–24.

Alvisi, Edoardo. *Nota al canto XI (versi 43–75) del "Paradiso" di Dante Alighieri*. Città di Castello: S. Lapi, 1894.

Ammann, Albert Maria. "Darstellung und Deutung der Sophia im vorpetrinischen Rußland." *Orientalia Christiana Periodica* 4 (1938): 120–156.

Ancona, Alessandro d'. *Scritti danteschi*. Florence: G. C. Sansoni, 1912.

Arquillière, Henri Xavier. *Le Plus Ancien Traité de l'Eglise: Jacques de Viterbo "De regimine christiano."* Paris: G. Beauchesne, 1926.

Auerbach, Erich. *Mimesis: The Representation of Reality in Western Literature*. Translated by Willard R. Trask. Princeton: Princeton University Press, 1953.

———. *Dante: Poet of the Secular World*. Translated by R. Manheim. Chicago: University of Chicago Press, 1961.

Balić, Carlo. "The Mediaeval Controversy over the Immaculate Conception up to the Death of Scotus." In *The Dogma of the Immaculate Conception: History and Significance*, 161–212. Edited by Edward Dennis O'Connor. Notre Dame: University of Notre Dame Press, 1958.

Baltes, Matthias. "Gott, Welt, Mensch in der 'Consolatio Philosophiae' des Boethius." *Vigiliae Christianae* 34 (1980):313–340.

Bambeck, Manfred. *Studien zu Dantes "Paradiso."* Wiesbaden: Steiner, 1979.

Barbi, Michele. *Life of Dante*. Translated by P. Ruggiers. Berkeley: University of California Press, 1954.

Barré, H. "Saint Bernard, docteur marial." In *Saint Bernard théologien*, 92–113. Rome: Analecta Sacri Ordinis Cisterciensis, 1953.

Barrett, Helen M. *Boethius: Some Aspects of His Times and Work*. Cambridge: Cambridge University Press, 1940.

Bäumer, Gertrud. *Die drei göttlichen Komödien des Abendlandes: Wolframs Parsifal, Dantes Divina Commedia, Goethes Faust*. Münster: Regensberg, 1949.

Bergin, Thomas Goddard. *Il canto IX del Paradiso*. Rome: A. Signorelli, 1959.

———. *Dante*. New York: Orion Press, 1965.

———. *Boccaccio*. New York: Viking Press, 1981.

Betti, Ugo. *Religione e teatro, il canto XXIX del Paradiso*. Brescia: Marcelliana, 1957.

Blaise, Albert, and Henri Chirat. *Dictionnaire latin-français des auteurs chrétiens*. Strasbourg: Le Latin Chrétien, 1954.

Bosco, Umberto, ed. *Enciclopedia Dantesca*. 6 vols. Rome: Istituto della Enciclopedia Italiana, 1970–1978.

Bover, José Maria. "Maria Mediatrix." *Ephemerides Theologicae Lovanienses* 6 (1929):439–462.

Brandeis, Irma., ed. *Discussions of the Divine Comedy*. Boston: D. C. Heath, 1961.

Burckhardt, Jacob. *The Civilization of the Renaissance in Italy*. Translated by S. G. C. Middlemore; introductions by Benjamin Nelson and Charles Trinkaus. 2 vols. New York: Harper Torchbooks, 1958.

Burdach, Konrad. "Die humanistischen Wirkungen der 'Trostschrift' des Boethius im Mittelalter und in der Renaissance." *Deutsche Vierteljahrschrift für Literaturwissenschaft und Geistesgeschichte* 11 (1933):530–558.

Busnelli, Giovanni. *Il concetto e l'ordine del "Paradiso" dantesco: Indagini e studii*. Città di Castello: S. Lapi, 1911.

Capetti, Vittorio. *Studi di Paradiso dantesco. Con un'appendice: Dante e le legende di S. Pier Damiani*. Bologna: Biblioteca Storico-Critica della Letteratura Dantesca, 1906.

Carroll, John S. *In Patriam: An Exposition of Dante's "Paradiso."* Glasgow: Hodder and Stoughton, 1911.

Case, Shirley Jackson. *The Origins of Christian Supernaturalism*. Chicago: University of Chicago Press, 1946.

Chadwick, Henry. *Boethius: The Consolations of Music, Logic, Theology and Philosophy*. Oxford: Clarendon Press, 1981.

Chamberlain, D. S. "Philosophy of Music in the *Consolation* of Boethius." *Speculum* 45 (1970):80–97.

Chiavacci Leonardi, Anna M. *Lettura del Paradiso dantesco.* Florence: Sansoni, 1963.

Chierici, Joseph. *L'aquila d'oro nel cielo di Giove: Canti XVIII–XX del Paradiso.* Rome: Istituto Grafico Tiberino, 1962.

Cooper, Lane, ed. *A Concordance of Boethius: The Five Theological Tractates and the "Consolation of Philosophy."* Cambridge, Mass.: Mediaeval Academy of America, 1928.

Cordati Martinelli, Bruna. *Lettura scolastica dell terza cantica.* Pisa: Nistri-Lischi, 1967.

Cornford, Francis M. *Plato's Cosmology: The "Timaeus" of Plato Translated with a Running Commentary.* New York: Liberal Arts Press, 1957.

Cosmo, Umberto. *L'ultima ascesa: Introduzione alla lettura del Paradiso.* Bari: G. Laterza e Figli, 1936.

———. *A Handbook to Dante Studies.* Translated by David Moore. Oxford: Oxford University Press, 1950.

Courcelle, Pierre. "Etude critique sur les commentaires de la 'Consolation' de Boèce (IXᵉ–XVᵉ siècles)." *Archives d'Histoire Doctrinale et Littéraire du Moyen Age* 14 (1939):5–140.

———. *La Consolation de philosophie dans la tradition littéraire: Antécédents et Posterité de Boèce.* Paris: Etudes Augustiniennes, 1967.

D'Amato, Juliana. "La corde e Gerione: un'altra interpretazione della famosa corda." In *Studies in Honor of Tatiana Fotitch,* 191–201. Washington, D.C.: Catholic University of America Press, 1972.

Di Scipio, Giuseppe C. *The Symbolic Rose in Dante's "Paradiso."* Ravenna: Longo, 1984.

Dronke, Peter. *Dante and Medieval Latin Traditions.* Paperback edition. Cambridge: Cambridge University Press, 1988.

Dunbar, H. F. *Symbolism in Medieval Thought and Its Consummation in the Divine Comedy.* New Haven: Yale University Press, 1929.

Fiero, Gloria K., Wendy Pfeffer, and Mathé Allain, *Three Medieval Views of Women.* New Haven: Yale University Press, 1989.

Foster, Kenelm. "Gli elogi danteschi di S. Francesco e di S. Domenico." In *Dante e il Francescanesimo,* 229–249. Cava dei Tirreni: Avagliano, 1987.

Freccero, John, ed. *Dante: A Collection of Critical Essays*. Englewood Cliffs, N. J.: Prentice-Hall, 1965.

———. "Dante's Prologue Scene." *Dante Studies* 84, ed. Anthony Pellegrini. Cambridge, Mass.: Dante Society of America, 1966.

———. *Dante: Poetics of Conversion*. Cambridge, Mass.: Harvard University Press, 1986.

Gardner, Edmund Garratt. *Dante's Ten Heavens: A Study of the "Paradiso."* London: A. Constable and Company, 1904.

Gewirth, Alan. *Marsilius of Padua and Medieval Political Philosophy*. New York: Columbia University Press, 1951.

Giamatti, Angelo Bartlett. *The Earthly Paradise and the Renaissance Epic*. Princeton: Princeton University Press, 1966.

Gibbon, Edward. *The History of the Decline and Fall of the Roman Empire*. Edited by John Bagnell Bury. 7 vols. London: Methuen and Co., 1896–1900.

Gibson, Margaret, ed. *Boethius: His Life, Thought and Influence*. Oxford: Basil Blackwell, 1981.

Gilson, Etienne. "Pourquoi saint Thomas a critiqué saint Augustin." *Archives d'Histoire Doctrinale et Littéraire du Moyen Age* 1 (1926): 5–127.

———. *The Mystical Theology of Saint Bernard*. Translated by A.H.C. Downes. New York: Sheed and Ward, 1940.

———. *Dante the Philosopher*. Translated by David Moore. New York: Sheed and Ward, 1949.

———. *A Gilson Reader*. Edited by Anton C. Pegis. Garden City, N.Y.: Hanover House, 1957.

Graef, Hilda. *Mary: A History of Doctrine and Devotion*. 2 vols. London and New York: Sheed and Ward, 1963–1965.

Grasso, Vincenzo. *Il "De consolatione philosophiae" di Boezio in Dante, Petrarca, Chaucer*. Catania: Vincenzo Muglia, 1923.

Gruber, Joachim. *Kommentar zu Boethius "De Consolatione Philosophiae."* Berlin: De Gruyter, 1978.

Guzzo, Augusto. *Il Cristianesimo nel "Paradiso" di Dante*. Turin: Edizioni di "Filosofia," 1959.

Harrower, Rachel Blanche. *A New Theory of Dante's Matelda*. Cambridge: Cambridge University Press, 1926.

Iorio, Giovanni. *Il canto IX del Paradiso*. Rome: A. Signorelli, 1969.

Kantorowicz, Ernst H. *The King's Two Bodies: A Study in Mediaeval Political Theology*. Princeton: Princeton University Press, 1957.

Kennan, Elizabeth T. "The 'De Consideratione' of St. Bernard of

Clairvaux in the Mid-Twelfth Century: A Review of Scholarship." *Traditio* 23 (1967):73–115.

Lambert, Malcolm David. *Franciscan Poverty: The Doctrine of the Absolute Poverty of Christ and the Apostles in the Franciscan Order, 1220–1323*. London: S.P.C.K., 1961.

Lampe, Geoffrey. *A Patristic Greek Lexicon*. Oxford: Clarendon Press, 1961.

Leclercq, Jean. *Saint Bernard mystique*. Paris: Desclée de Brouwer, 1948.

————. *The Love of Learning and the Desire for God: A Study of Monastic Culture*. Translated by Catharine Misrahi. New York: Fordham University Press, 1961.

————. *La Femme et les femmes dans l'œuvre de Saint Bernard*. Paris: Tequi, 1982.

Lewis, Clive Staples. *The Allegory of Love: A Study in Mediaeval Tradition*. Oxford: Oxford University Press, 1951.

Lovejoy, Arthur O. *The Great Chain of Being. A Study of the History of an Idea*. Cambridge, Mass.: Harvard University Press, 1936.

Lovera, Luciano, ed. *Concordanza della Commedia di Dante Alighieri*. 3 vols. Turin: Giulio Einaudi, 1975.

Lubac, Henri de. *The Eternal Feminine: A Study on the Poem by Teilhard de Chardin*. Translated by René Hague. London: Collins, 1971.

Maccarone, Michele. "Teologia e diritto canonico nella *Monarchia*, III, 3." *Rivista di Storia della Chiesa in Italia* 5 (1951).

McKeon, Richard P. "Aristotelianism in Western Christianity." In *Environmental Factors in Christian History*, 206–231. Edited by John T. McNeill et al. Chicago: University of Chicago Press, 1939.

Mandelbaum, Allen. *The Divine Comedy of Dante Alighieri: A Verse Translation with Introduction and Commentary*. 3 vols. Berkeley and Los Angeles: University of California Press, 1980–1984.

Mandonnet, Pierre. *Dante le théologien: Introduction à l'intelligence de la vie, des œuvres et de l'art de Dante Alighieri*. Paris: Desclée de Brouwer, 1935.

Marchese, Angelo. *Guida alla Divina commedia: Paradiso*. Turin: Società Editrice Internazionale, 1980.

Masseron, Alexandre. *Dante et Saint Bernard*. Paris: A. Michel, 1953.

Mazzeo, Joseph Anthony. *Structure and Thought in the "Paradiso."* Ithaca: Cornell University Press, 1958.

Mazzotta, Giuseppe. *Dante: Poet of the Desert*. Princeton: Princeton University Press, 1979.

Moore, Edward. *Studies in Dante*. 4 vols. Oxford: Clarendon Press, 1896–1917.

Morison, Samuel Eliot. *Christopher Columbus, Mariner*. New York: New American Library, 1955.

Murari, Rocco. *Dante e Boezio: Contributo alla studio delle fonti dantesche*. Bologna: N. Zanichelli, 1905.

Musa, Mark. *Essays on Dante*. Bloomington: Indiana University Press, 1964.

Nardi, Bruno. *Nel mondo di Dante*. Rome: Edizioni di "Storia e Letteratura," 1944.

———. *Saggi di filosofia dantesca*. Florence: La Nuova Editrice, 1967.

Needler, Howard. *Saint Francis and Saint Dominic in the "Divine Comedy."* Krefeld: Scherpe Verlag, 1969.

Newman, Barbara. "Sergius Bulgakov and the Theology of Divine Wisdom." *St. Vladimir's Theological Quarterly* 22 (1978):39–73.

———. *Sister of Wisdom: St. Hildegard's Theology of the Feminine*. Berkeley: University of California Press, 1987.

Nuttall, Anthony David. *Overheard by God: Fiction and Prayer in Herbert, Milton, Dante, and St. John*. New York: Methuen, 1980.

Oakley, Francis. *The Western Church in the Later Middle Ages*. Ithaca: Cornell University Press, 1979.

Oberman, Heiko Augustinus. *Forerunners of the Reformation*. New York: Holt, Rinehart, and Winston, 1966.

Palgen, Rudolf. *Dantes Sternglaube: Beiträge zur Erklärung des Paradiso*. Heidelberg: C. Winter, 1940.

Paperini, Giovanni Filippo. *Lezione sopra Dante*. Città di Castello: S. Lapi, 1902.

Patch, Howard Rollin. *The Goddess Fortuna in Medieval Literature*. Cambridge, Mass.: Harvard University Press, 1927.

———. *The Tradition of Boethius: A Study of His Importance in Medieval Culture*. New York: Oxford University Press, 1935.

Pelikan, Jaroslav. *The Christian Tradition: A History of the Development of Doctrine*. 5 vols. Chicago: University of Chicago Press, 1971–1989.

———. "Mary—Exemplar of the Development of Christian Doctrine." In *Mary: Images of the Mother of Jesus in Jewish and Christian Perspective*, 79–91. Philadelphia: Fortress Press, 1986.

————. *The Mystery of Continuity: Time and History, Memory and Eternity in the Thought of Saint Augustine.* Charlottesville: University Press of Virginia, 1986.

Pépin, Jean. *Dante et la tradition de l'allégorie.* Montreal: Institut d'Etudes Médiévales, 1970.

Peterson, Erik. *The Angels and the Liturgy.* Translated by Ronald Walls. New York: Herder and Herder, 1964.

Rabuse, Georg. *Die goldene Leiter in Dantes Saturnhimmel.* Krefeld: Scherpe Verlag, 1972.

Ralphs, Sheila. *Etterno Spiro: A Study in the Nature of Dante's Paradise.* Manchester: Manchester University Press, 1959.

Rand, Edward Kennard. "On the Composition of Boethius' *Consolatio Philosophiae.*" *Harvard Studies in Classical Philology* 15 (1904): 1–28.

————. *Founders of the Middle Ages.* Cambridge, Mass.: Harvard University Press, 1928.

Reiss, Edmund. *Boethius.* Boston: Twayne, 1982.

Rivière, Jean. *Le Problème de l'église et de l'état au temps de Philippe le Bel.* Paris: E. Champion, 1926.

Santarelli, Giuseppe. *S. Francesco in Dante: Sintesi storico-critica.* Milan: Edizioni Francescane Cammino, 1969.

Scheible, Helga. *Die Gedichte in der "Consolatio Philosophiae" des Boethius.* Heidelberg: C. Winter, 1972.

Schnapp, Jeffrey Thompson. *The Transfiguration of History at the Center of Dante's Paradise.* Princeton: Princeton University Press, 1986.

Shapiro, Marianne. *Woman, Earthly and Divine, in the "Comedy" of Dante.* Lexington: University Press of Kentucky, 1975.

Shaw, James Eustace. *The Lady "Philosophy" in the "Convivio."* Cambridge, Mass.: Dante Society, 1938.

Shea, George W. "Outline History of Mariology in the Middle Ages and Modern Times." In *Mariology*, ed. Juniper B. Carol, 1:281–327. Milwaukee: Bruce Publishing Company, 1955.

Silk, Edward T. "Boethius' *Consolation of Philosophy* as a Sequel to Augustine's Dialogues and Soliloquies." *Harvard Theological Review* 32 (1939):19–39.

Sinclair, John D. *The "Divine Comedy" of Dante Alighieri: Italian Text with English Translation and Comment.* 3 vols. Galaxy Edition. New York: Oxford University Press, 1961.

Singleton, Charles S. *An Essay on the "Vita Nuova."* Cambridge, Mass.: Harvard University Press, 1949.

———, ed. *The Divine Comedy of Dante Alighieri.* 3 vols. Bollingen Edition. Princeton: Princeton University Press, 1982.

Smalley, Beryl. *The Study of the Bible in the Middle Ages.* Reprint edition. Notre Dame, Ind.: University of Notre Dame Press, 1964.

Southern, Richard William. *The Making of the Middle Ages.* New Haven: Yale University Press, 1953.

Strouse, Jean. *Alice James: A Biography.* Boston: Houghton Mifflin Company, 1980.

Taylor, Henry Osborn. *The Mediaeval Mind.* 2 vols. 4th ed. London: Macmillan and Co., 1938.

Toynbee, Paget. *Dante Alighieri: His Life and Works.* Edited by Charles S. Singleton. New York: Harper Torchbooks, 1965.

Vettori, Vittorio, ed. *Letture del Paradiso.* Milan: Marzorati, 1970.

Vogel, C. J. de. "The Problem of Philosophy and Christian Faith in Boethius' *Consolatio.*" *Romanitas et Christianitas: Studia Iano Henrico Waszink,* 357–370. Amsterdam: North-Holland, 1973.

Vossler, Karl. *Medieval Culture: An Introduction to Dante and His Times.* Translated by William Cranston Lawton. 2 vols. New York: Harcourt Brace and Company, 1929.

Weigelt, Curt H., ed. *Giotto.* Berlin and Leipzig: Deutsche Verlags–Anstalt Stuttgart, 1925.

Wolf, Christine. "Untersuchungen zum Krankheitsbild in dem ersten Buch der 'Consolatio philosophiae' des Boethius." *Rivista di Cultura Classica e Medievale* 6 (1964):213–223.